EFFECTIVE
EMPLOYEE
ORIENTATION

Linda A. Jerris

amacom

AMERICAN MANAGEMENT ASSOCIATION
THE WORKSMART SERIES

New York • Atlanta • Boston • Chicago • Kansas City • San Francisco • Washington, D.C.
Brussels • Toronto • Mexico City

Library of Congress Cataloging-in-Publication Data

Jerris, Linda A.
   Effective employee orientation / Linda A. Jerris.
     p. cm.
   Includes bibliographical references.
   ISBN 0-8144-7797-6
   1. Employee orientation. I. Title.
HF5549.5.I53J47 1993
658.3'1242—dc20   *93-9250*
                         CIP

Printing number

10 9 8 7 6 5 4 3 2 1

CONTENTS

PART III. ORIENTATION AS AN ONGOING ACTIVITY

PREFACE

A number of major issues are having an impact on the work force of the 1990s. One of the most significant is its changing demographics. By the year 2000, 25 million new workers will enter the labor force. Of these, 85 percent will be what we now refer to as minorities or protected classes—women, Hispanics, blacks, Asians, Native Americans, and Pacific Islanders. Only 15 percent of these new workers will be white men. Further, experts predict that the United States will rank seventh in global productivity by the year 2003.

Along with the changing face of the work force is a shift in values that is creating new attitudes toward work and family. Among younger workers, in particular, there is an emphasis on the individual, replacing the "organization man" mind-set.

Finally, there are changes in the basic nature of the employer/ employee relationship. The workplace has become increasingly litigious as greater numbers of employees have challenged company policies and procedures in the courts. It is thus more important than ever for employers to fully communicate to their employees the conditions of their employment and how they are expected to perform.

WHY YOU SHOULD ORIENT YOUR NEW EMPLOYEES

Against this backdrop emerge some very important reasons why you should orient new employees:

    • *To communicate the values and priorities of the organization.* Every company has its traditions, lore, culture and jargon, and history. What's more, employees want to feel that they are an integral part of their organizations and to be competent representatives of the ownership and management of the companies at which they work. In order to do so they need to be educated not only about the company's culture but also about the business pressures and marketplace position of the company.

• *To model good customer service behavior.* Whether the company manufactures a product or renders a service, the customer's experience is directly affected by the attitudes and behaviors of the employees. Stressing that fact to employees, no matter what their position, is the first step in ensuring that customers will be properly treated at every stage of their interaction with the company.

• *To control hiring and turnover costs.* C. M. Caldwell notes in *New Employee Orientation* that one out of every five employees—or approximately 80,000 people—starts a new job every workday. According to an article in *Training & Development Journal,* it costs an average of $6,000 to hire a new employee. Yet a study in Judith Stevens-Long's *Adult Life* indicates that 50 to 60 percent of employees leave after only seven months of employment.*

• *To foster positive attitudes.* For many businesses, it is critical that employees feel they are part of a team. When they do feel that way they are more apt to "sell" the company to the customers and the community.

• *To bring employees up to speed faster.* Employees are most receptive to new information during their first few days on the job. Providing a physically comfortable environment, a warm welcome, and a sense of security helps employees to feel valued, to learn quickly, and to make a positive contribution from the start.

• *To prevent misunderstandings.* The orientation period is a good time to make sure that employees' expectations of

*C. M. Caldwell, *New Employee Orientation: A Practical Guide for Supervisors* (Los Altos, Calif.: Crisp Publications, 1988); Zandy B. Leibowitz, Nancy K. Schlossberg, and Jane E. Shore, "Stopping the Revolving Door," *Training & Development Journal* (February 1991); Judith Stevens-Long, *Adult Life: Development Processes* (Mountain View, Calif.: Mayfield Publishing, 1988).

the job are in line with their actual responsibilities and that there will be no surprises. Establishing the lines of communication from the beginning results in:

— Improved employee morale
— Better relationships between employees and managers
— Fewer employee errors on the job
— Better customer service
— Clearer understanding of company policies, procedures, and benefits

• *To protect the long-term health of the organization.* Orientation is, in effect, an investment that yields dividends in the form of lower turnover, lower costs, and a greater competitive edge.

You may often hear the terms *orientation* and *training* used as if they were synonymous. Although it is sometimes difficult to know exactly where one begins and the other ends, it is important for you to recognize the distinction between them and to understand that their objectives differ.

Orientation is the formal introduction of the new person to the organization and to the job.

Orientation is the formal introduction of the new person to the organization and to the job. Orientation answers the "what" questions new employees have on their first day of work: What is my new boss's name and the names of my co-workers? What hours do I work? What are the rules and regulations and policies and procedures I need to know? What papers do I sign to get my benefits, my paycheck, and so on? Orientation helps new employees get their bearings by pointing them in the right direction.

Training is on-the-job experience and information that help employees become more proficient or qualified at a task and prepare them for possible promotion to positions of greater responsibility or complexity. Training deals with the "how's"—how to be a better manager, how to master Lotus 1-2-3, how to more quickly assemble wire harnesses, and the like.

This book approaches orientation as an ongoing process that supports the business objectives of the company and fosters high employee morale. New employees come to your company with great expectations, whether they be homemakers entering the work force for the first time, new graduates fresh from business school, or seasoned senior executives. They are eager to make a contribution immediately; therefore, it is critical that this eagerness not be dampened. Welcoming new employees and making them feel that their contribution is enthusiastically anticipated have strong and lasting effects on their productivity and their attitudes toward the job.

In general, creating a good first impression and getting new employees in synch with the company's culture, goals, and work environment is the responsibility of everyone in the organization. More specifically, top-level managers carry out their responsibility by deciding what kinds of orientation new employees should participate in, by approving expenditures, and by conveying their belief in the value of the orientation program down the line in the company. Line managers and supervisors, because they actually work with the new employees, have the most to gain from the orientation program and must be responsible for making sure that new employees know their jobs and the standards expected.

The overall success of an orientation program requires that one individual or one company unit be responsible for developing, implementing, and coordinating the program on an ongoing basis. In companies that have an established human resources function, that individual is usually the human resources representative. In companies that do not have a human resources department, line managers and supervisors may be the responsible individuals.

If yours is a company with a human resources department, your role as the human resources representative and that of your department will be to work in close liaison with the line managers to decide what information to communicate to new employees and which persons are best suited to communicate it.

This book will help you to determine what that relevant information is and how to convey it. You will learn:

- The necessary preliminaries to help you to develop an orientation program that suits the needs and priorities of your organization
- The elements of an effective orientation program
- How to design an orientation program
- How to conduct an orientation program

You may already have an orientation program in place but find, as many professionals do, that it does not work as well as you would like it to. Perhaps you have noticed some of the following conditions, any one of which signals that your program probably needs to be rethought or revised:

- Turnover at your company is low, and because employees are hired so infrequently, orientation has been done sporadically or not at all.
- You or others present the program so automatically that you feel you could do it in your sleep.
- Your program materials are outdated, as reflected in the styles of dress, decor, and individuals featured.
- You have never sought feedback from participants and you are not sure that the program addresses what it should.
- Managers in your company do not conduct departmental orientations on a regular basis.
- Your current program is too canned and does not really fit the personality of your company.
- Attendance at orientation sessions is low.
- Your program is cumbersome, involving too many videos, modules, and lengthy written materials, and results in a lack of interest and support.
- Your program follows a conventional presentation format and does not meet the needs of disabled employees.

You can use this book as a back-to-basics guide to creating a more workable orientation program.

PART

I

THE WHAT AND WHY OF ORIENTATION

CHAPTER 1

ORIENTATION: A PROCESS, NOT JUST A PROGRAM

Often the word orientation conjures up images of stacks of materials to read, endless forms to fill out, lectures that seem to go on forever (or, as one employee put it, "borientation"), or, at the opposite extreme, being shown a desk and the location of the rest room and then put to work immediately.

New employees remember their first day of work for years, so for the lasting impression to be a good one, it must be well-managed. This means that rather than looking at an orientation program as a series of activities or tasks, you should look at it as a total process that fits in with the overall business activities of your company.

Formulating a strategic business plan involves deciding the company's mission—its continuing purpose or reason for being. The company then formulates the goals and objectives that will help it to achieve that mission. Your company's strategic plan provides the framework for a successful orientation program.

Creating a first-class orientation program and process is a job worth doing and doing well.

—RON ZEMKE

Just as the strategic planning is a lengthy process, you can expect that planning and developing your orientation program will take a considerable amount of time and research. This expenditure of time and effort is necessary to create a program that fits with your company's strategic plan and meets the real needs of your company.

You should consider doing the following as you develop your program:

3

**Under-
stand the
culture of
the new
company
and its
standards
of what is
reasonable.**

—JAMES C.
NUNAN

1. *Aligning the program with the company's mission statement.* For example, a major insurance company has as one of its key business activities a focus on customer service. The company centers its employee orientation program around the theme QUALITY FROM THE START. QUALITY FROM THE START is based on practices that cluster around the following three areas of on-the-job action:

- Quality and customer focus. The excellent employee:
  —Knows who his or her customer is.
  —Is service-and results-oriented.
  —Completes projects right the first time, and on time.
  —Demonstrates high personal standards.
  —Pursues self-development.
- Accountability for results. The excellent employee:
  —Is personally accountable for high-quality results and takes responsibility for getting the job done.
  —Demonstrates a sense of urgency in completing tasks.
  —Asks questions, finds out why, and is curious.
  —Is decisive.
- Teamwork. The excellent employee:
  —Communicates with associates, management, and customers.
  —Shares ideas and sells new ideas.

2. *Setting significant, measurable goals and objectives that reflect the unique needs of your company.* They should articulate your expectations of the program, and be capable of serving as a benchmark for following up and refining the program. For example, if one of your company's objectives is to win an award such as the Malcolm Baldrige National Quality Award) or industry distinction ("endorsed by the American Medical Association"), the strategic plan for your orientation program must focus on activities that move you toward that objective.

3. *Emphasizing a solid orientation as essential to improving and maintaining productivity and profits.* New employees want and *need* to know early on (usually within the first thirty

days of employment) about the company, its objectives, values, marketplace position, and where they, their departments, and their jobs fit into the total picture. Orientation helps new employees understand their role within the organization and the impact of their contribution. As a result, they become productive sooner and are less likely to look for jobs elsewhere.

4. *Involving senior management.* Besides setting policy and approving expenditures, top-level managers provide support and endorsement and set the tone for enthusiastic acceptance of the orientation program by the whole organization. At a Philadelphia-based hospital corporation, new employee orientation is conducted by the vice-president of human resources as evidence that the administration values the orientation program. Numerous articles have highlighted how the success of the orientation programs at Texas Instruments and Corning Incorporated were largely due to the work done by management steering committees and advisory groups.

5. *Making line managers and supervisors key in the orientation process.* Line managers and supervisors work hands-on with new employees to make sure that they know the job and the standards expected, the work environment, and what the employee can expect from the company. They have the most influence on employees' initial experiences and on their future success potential.

6. *Fostering two-way communication between new employees and top management.* An example of this is an Atlanta bank that for over ten years has emphasized the accessibility of top executives and has encouraged the asking of questions in its orientation program. The president encourages new employees to talk with him if they have problems; employees who have taken the president at his word have found that he is sincere. At the orientation session of a multihealth care corporation, the president speaks about the company's history, current status, and future plans. Participants are asked beforehand, "If you could ask the company president one question, what would it be?" These questions are submitted

to the president to provide an initial list of questions and to prompt additional questions from the audience.

7. *Conducting ongoing follow-up and review.* You must frequently review your program to determine whether you are meeting your goals and objectives and, if you are not, make the necessary adjustments. Indicators by which to measure the success of your orientation program include:

- Impact on turnover
- Length of time it takes new employees to learn
- Quality of session content and delivery
- Attendance at sessions
- Effectiveness of entire system

CHAPTER 2

DEVELOPING YOUR PROGRAM

"I never knew I was supposed to do it that way."

"When I arrived at work the first day, they didn't even have a desk for me, let alone anything to do."

"I just couldn't believe that my new boss, the person I was supposed to be working for, didn't even come over and say hello."

If this is some of the feedback you have gotten about your new employees' first day on the job, there is no doubt that your orientation program needs help. However, your first step in developing a program may involve convincing management that orienting new employees actually protects its investment in employee benefits and in the new employees themselves.

Convincing management often requires a great deal of supporting evidence. Good sources for this include your colleagues—senior managers, line managers, and supervisors; line employees; external customers; and other companies. You can obtain information through interviews, surveys, and focus groups to help you determine:

- The purpose of your orientation program.
- The specific information new employees need to know and when that information should be presented.
- The best methods to get the information across to new employees.

GETTING THE INFORMATION

One-on-one interviews and focus groups have the advantage of enabling you to get immediate feedback from participants and to build personal relationships. Participants often assign high value and importance to the questions asked. However, personal interviews and focus groups do require much planning and coordination to maximize the value of the time spent doing them.

Survey questionnaires are more confidential, simpler to administer—particularly if multiple sites are involved—and can be completed at any time. However, they do require more of your time to follow up and make sure that they are completed *and* returned. Not everyone likes to take the time to complete them.

You can maximize participant receptivity to your information gathering and ensure reliable and consistent information if you prepare appropriate questions ahead of time. Keep in mind that your questions must be designed from the perspective of the individuals being surveyed. Your approach with senior management should be "big picture"; line managers' and supervisors' questions should relate to their roles and functions in their own departments. Employees should be surveyed from the perspective of their individual jobs. Customers' questions should relate to their perceptions of the quality of the delivery of the company's product or service. Some sample questions follow.

For Senior Management

1. Why are we orienting our new employees? What are our key objectives?
2. What overall picture of the organization do we want new employees to take away from the orientation session (for example, that we're on the cutting edge of technology, that people are important to our business, that our approach to doing business is conservative)?

3. What specific topics or areas are critical for new employees to understand (for example, company objectives, the rewards and recognition system, obligations to the customer)?

4. How will we know that the objectives of the orientation program have been met? What standards should be set and what period of time should pass before we evaluate the results of the orientation program against those standards?

5. How much time and effort can be invested in the design of the program? And in the implementation program?

6. What will it cost? What will be our ROI (return on investment) in terms of productivity, lower turnover, increased sales?

7. What are the best ways of conveying the value of the orientation program to our managers and obtaining adequate support from them?

For Line Managers and Supervisors

1. What are the key work attitudes that new employees should bring to their jobs?

2. What are some of the obstacles new employees are confronted with on their first day of work? their first week?

3. What suggestions can you make to help the new employee feel comfortable on the job and become productive quickly?

4. What is the most effective method of conveying the information employees need to have?

5. When is the best time for new employees to attend an orientation session?

6. What is the most critical introductory information that new employees in your department need to have (for example, how the department is organized, who the key personnel are, the location of supplies or tools)?

7. Are there any special characteristics or needs of your

work force or department that ought to be considered (for example, literacy situations that would require using visual orientation materials to a greater extent than requiring reading, a focus on career paths within the company in the program content, scheduling of orientation so that there is adequate coverage during busy times)?

8. Describe a behavior or behaviors that signal to you that a new employee is fully oriented.

For Employees

1. As a member of [department], what exactly do you do at your job?
2. What are your overall goals as a professional in this job?
3. What are the obstacles that keep you from performing your job to the best of your ability?
4. When confronted with a problem on the job, whom do you ask for help in solving it?
5. Do you feel important at your job? What makes you feel important?
6. Do you know what is expected of you on your job?
7. How do you find out what is going on in the company?
8. What services or products do we provide to our customers?
9. Are you clear about what company benefits are available to you and how to obtain them?
10. Indicate below to what extent your day-to-day experiences and tasks on the job are in line with your expectations of the job when you were hired:
    ☐ Exactly what I expected
    ☐ Somewhat different from what I expected
    ☐ Not at all what I expected
    Explain: _____
11. What are the three most important things about the company a new employee should know?

INCLUDING YOUR CUSTOMERS IN THE SURVEY

Many companies have found that quality customer service makes the difference between building a customer's loyalty or losing that customer forever. Companies that have ignored customer service have especially felt the crunch from competitors. By contrast, companies that have devoted time and resources to making sure that their customers are satisfied have expanded and flourished.

> **Quality is never an accident; it is always the result of intelligent effort.**
>
> **—JOHN RUSKIN**

A common characteristic of organizations that succeed in satisfying their customers is that their employees are aware of the priority that the company places on creating and maintaining high levels of customer service. Employees need to understand their service roles and pass along company values and aspirations about service. Frontline employees in particular often do not have as clear a picture as their managers have of the company's strategies and standards for customer service.

The orientation program is the ideal vehicle for communicating such standards, and your customers are the ideal source of information in formulating what those standards should be. See the box on page 12 for a customer questionnaire.

FEEDBACK FROM OTHER COMPANIES

When you survey other companies about their orientation programs, you can use the open-ended questions in the box on page 13 as a guide.

COMPILING YOUR SURVEY RESULTS

Once you've gathered and analyzed the data you can proceed in one of two ways, depending on the amount of authority

(Text continues on page 14.)

Knowledge is the only instrument of production that is not subject to diminishing returns.

—JOHN MAURICE CLARK

CUSTOMER QUESTIONNAIRE

We appreciate your business and want you to be satisifed with every aspect of your experience with our company. Our highest priority is to provide you with a high level of service, and we would like to know if there are areas of our service that need improvement. This questionnaire is intended to help us evaluate our performance and to make any adjustments that appear necessary. Please take a moment to read the following statements and tell us where you think our service rates on a scale of 1 to 5 (5 = excellent, 4 = above average, 3 = good, 2 = fair, 1 = poor).

1. When our company promises to do something by a certain time, it does so.   5 4 3 2 1

2. When you have a problem, our company shows a sincere interest in solving it.   5 4 3 2 1

3. Our company performs the service right the first time.   5 4 3 2 1

4. Our records are always accurate.   5 4 3 2 1

5. Our employees give you prompt service.   5 4 3 2 1

6. Our employees demonstrate a willingness to help you.   5 4 3 2 1

7. The behavior of our employees instills confidence in you.   5 4 3 2 1

8. You feel safe in your business dealings with our company.   5 4 3 2 1

9. Our employees are consistently courteous with you.   5 4 3 2 1

10. Our employees understand your specific needs.   5 4 3 2 1

11. You receive personal attention from our employees.   5 4 3 2 1

12. Our employees have the knowledge needed to answer your questions.   5 4 3 2 1

13. No employee is ever too busy to respond to your request.   5 4 3 2 1

OTHER COMPANY QUESTIONNAIRE

1. How did you decide what the goals and objectives of your orientation program would be?

2. Does your program focus on a philosophy, theme, or slogan?

3. What are some of the concepts or principles that your program is based on?

4. Do you make a distinction between orientation and training?

5. Are there specific questions you ask applicants during the job interview that help you to determine whether or not they have realistic expectations of what the job entails?

6. What information do you give applicants about your company during the interview?

7. How soon after being hired are employees oriented?

8. How frequently do you hold orientation sessions (weekly, monthly)?

9. How long is an orientation session (full day, half day)?

10. What is your overall timetable for the new employee's orientation? Does the orientation extend beyond the first day of work?

11. What delivery methods and audiovisuals do you use?

12. What topics/areas of priority do you cover in the orientation?

13. Do you have a departmental orientation? What is covered?

14. To what extent are line and senior managers involved in the design or delivery of the orientation program?

15. Do you conduct follow-up orientations? If so, how soon after the initial orientation do you conduct the follow-up? What information do you cover?

16. What accommodations do you make for people with special needs, for example, people with disabilities or insufficient command of English?

17. Do you solicit employee feedback on the orientation program?

18. Does your company handbook have a written orientation policy?

and responsibility you have been given for developing the orientation program.

If you have been charged with gathering information only for review by top management, your next step is to present a preliminary proposal outlining your recommendations for the structure of a program. An example of such a proposal is in the box on pages 15–16.

If you have been assigned total responsibility for the orientation program, you should develop goals and objectives, which become the program's blueprint. Goals define the overall results you want from your program; objectives describe the specific ways in which you can achieve the overall goals of the program and are expressed by what you want participants to do after completing the program.

Here are some typical goals and objectives.

Goals

1. To welcome new employees, relieve their anxieties, and make them feel at home.
2. To develop rapport between the company and new employees and make them feel a part of the organization as quickly as possible.
3. To inspire new employees with a good attitude toward the company and the job.
4. To acquaint new employees with the goals, history, management, traditions, policies, departments, divisions, products, and physical layout of the organization.
5. To communicate to new employees what is expected of them, what their responsibilities are, and how they should handle themselves.
6. To present the basic information employees want to know concerning rules and regulations, benefits, payday, procedures, and general practices.
7. To encourage a spirit of inquiry in new employees, show them how to learn, and assist them in the acquisition of additional knowledge and skills.

AN ORIENTATION PROGRAM PROPOSAL FOR NBT CORPORATION

Introduction

NBT Corporation hires an average of 50 to 100 technical staff and 200 entry-level staff per year at our headquarters location. We estimate that the cost for each new hire is $30,000 to $40,000 per person per year. The cost for each entry-level person is estimated to be $10,000. In the past three years, 30 to 50 percent of the new hires have left during their first year of employment, just as they were beginning to learn their jobs. This has caused declines in productivity and profits.

Based on the results of several surveys that were conducted over the past six months (see "Survey Results" section), it has become clear that we need a better and more systematic way of helping new employees to become acclimated to the company and to their new jobs.

The Survey

From January until approximately mid-June of this year a survey of all senior executives, line managers, and supervisors was conducted. New and current employees and customers were also surveyed and were selected to participate at random.

The detailed results appear in the Appendix section of this proposal. Below is a summary:

1. Senior executives overwhelmingly agree that our orientation program should build a positive attitude toward the company, elicit a commitment from our employees to company goals, and, as a priority, increase employee productivity. Most executives felt that one year would be a reasonable time period in which to put an orientation program in place and that the expense would be recovered in six months through reduced turnover.
2. Eighty percent of line managers felt that employees should be familiar with the basic parts of their jobs within three months. In the production area, key job skills included being able to read blueprints and troubleshoot equipment. In the customer service area, product knowledge and the ability to "turn difficult customers around" were cited.
3. The survey indicated that improvement needs to be made in customer service, especially product knowledge. About 25 percent of the customer respondents said that our

(continues)

customer service staff people conveyed an "I don't care" attitude.

4. The majority of new employees indicated frustration with the disorganized nature of their introduction to the company. Several longer-term employees indicated that they still do not have a full understanding of what their jobs are all about.

Conclusions

The results of the survey indicate that the focus in developing a new employee orientation program should probably be in the areas of:

- Communicating company goals and objectives
- Customer service skills
- Product knowledge
- Job knowledge

Next Steps

It is recommended that a steering committee be formed to design and develop an orientation program and that top management and line managers be represented on the committee. The steering committee, coordinated by the human resources department, would be responsible for the following:

- More in-depth research as to how areas of concern should be addressed by the orientation program
- Program objectives
- Program budget
- Content development and determination of how it is to be delivered
- Production of all materials used in the program
- Piloting the program
- Training supervisors to deliver sessions
- Evaluating feedback and results and appropriate fine-tuning of the program

Summary

Based on survey feedback, we need a systematic orientation if we are going to reduce turnover, shorten the time it takes for new employees to learn their jobs, ensure that all new employees receive consistent information, and render a higher level of service to our customers.

8. To provide the basic skills, terms, and ideas of the business world and help new employees in human relations.

9. To convey to new employees the importance of their jobs to the overall success of the company and to make them feel a part of the team from the first day of work.

10. To impress upon new employees the importance of their roles in ensuring complete customer satisfaction.

Objectives

1. Post memos on employee bulletin board announcing the new employee's name and department no later than three days before the employee reports to work.

2. Enroll new employee in next scheduled orientation session within one week of his/her start date.

3. Review company organization chart and position new players in their respective departments.

4. Send welcome letter signed by the President to the home of each new employee.

5. Have specific, manageable assignments ready for the new employee on the first day of work.

6. Enroll all customer contact employees in "You: A Service Professional" within the first month of employment.

7. Send a follow-up questionnaire to the new employee one month after the formal orientation session and direct him/her to complete and return it to the human resources department to ascertain how much program information has been retained.

8. Run a feature story about the new employee(s) in the next regularly scheduled in-house newsletter.

9. Have the relevant supervisor review the orientation checklist with the new employee and return it to the Human Resources Department for filing in the employee's personnel file within one month of employment.

SIMPLE CORPORATE ORIENTATION POLICY

All newly hired personnel will receive orientation to the company and to their specific assignments, regardless of position or level of prior experience. The orientation will be planned, implemented, and evaluated to ensure that each employee is provided the opportunity to develop his or her potential to perform at a level of excellence consistent with the performance standards established in every operational area. The manager of each operation is responsible for ensuring that this policy is carried out.

Orientation will be scheduled on a regular basis. Under no circumstances will an employee be placed at a workstation with no orientation.

DETAILED CORPORATE ORIENTATION POLICY

Each new employee is to receive proper orientation, that is, information, instruction, and guidance from both the human resources department and the employee's immediate supervisor.
The human resources department is responsible for discussing the following areas:

- ☐ Group life insurance program
- ☐ Shift premium payment and overtime premium payment provision
- ☐ Union membership requirements
- ☐ Payday information
- ☐ Parking lot use regulations
- ☐ Health and first-aid policies, including whom to call when sick
- ☐ Smoking policies
- ☐ Wages and the wage plan
- ☐ New employee probationary period

The supervisor's role in the orientation process for hourly employees is divided into these categories:

- ☐ Introduction to department supervisors and employees and brief explanation of what other employees do and their relationship to the new employee's job; identification of facilities such as the coatroom, rest rooms, drinking fountain, supply cabinet, production area, computers, and so forth.
- ☐ General instructions concerning work schedule, breaks, lunch, wash-up periods, production standards, and the availability of supervisors to handle problems and questions.

☐ Health and safety discussions concerning safety precautions on the job; use of protective equipment such as gloves, goggles, and respirators; and fire protection procedures, use of alarm boxes, extinguishers, and blankets, and smoking regulations.

☐ Instructions on how to do the job, the new employee's role in the operation, follow-up and evaluation of job performance, and in-service training as necessary.

10. Conduct a tour of the facility and of the new employee's department on the first day of work.

11. On the first day of work, assign to new employees a "buddy" to introduce them to others with whom they will be working.

12. Provide new employees with brochures outlining benefits, pay, the performance review system, and basic company policies and procedures.

ESTABLISHING AN ORIENTATION POLICY

A commitment to orientation involves a willingness to invest time, effort, and resources to construct and maintain the program.

A commitment to orientation involves a willingness to invest time, effort, and resources to construct and maintain the program. The emphasis is on investment. Spending money on a well-designed and well-executed program results in a long-range return on investment through improved employee productivity.

To support this commitment, it is important that the company articulate its orientation policy in writing beyond merely stating that "We believe in orientation." The actual wording of your policy will depend on the nature of your business; what is more important is that a policy be written and be made part of your standard operating procedures. See the box on pages 18–19 for a simple and more detailed policy statement.

CHAPTER 3

TAILORING YOUR PROGRAM TO YOUR WORK FORCE

Each employee brings to the job a different type and level of experience, ability to learn and grow, and limitations.

As noted previously, today's work force is more diverse than ever before—in terms of its cultural variety, physical capabilities, and the work life stages and ages represented. Each employee brings to the job a different type and level of experience, ability to learn and grow, and limitations. As you begin to create your orientation program, you must keep in mind who your work force is so that you can design a program that is relevant to these real people.

This does not mean that a different program is needed for every type of employee. It does mean that developing a process for smoothly integrating new employees into your company requires an understanding of the values and expectations these new employees bring to the company and a determination of where your primary focus should be in making them feel noticed, appreciated, and valued.

Let's look first at some of the employees who comprise the work force and at their expectations and values.

EMPLOYEES NEW TO THE WORK FORCE

Employees new to the work force are often college students needing assistance in making the transition from the academic world to the business world. For some, the new job may also be their first. The most significant aspect of dealing with these employees is understanding how their work-related attitudes and expectations differ from those of the previous "corporation man" generation of college graduates of the 1950s and 1960s. College graduates of the 1990s are less likely to have climbing the corporate pyramid as life's goal. Having come of age in an environment of downsizing, stiff competition, and shifting corporate priorities, these people expect each job to help them develop a portfolio of skills that will ensure their future marketability to other companies or other industries. Their limited loyalty to one company, deserved or undeserved, is expressed in the words of a communications company management trainee: "I would leave this company tomorrow if I found a job that offered me a greater career opportunity. I do what my company pays me to do, but I know that if business warrants it, I'm gone."

Despite independent attitudes and lack of allegiance to any one company, their limited experience and uncertainty about workplace behavior in the real world make them the most impressionable work group. They often refuse to admit that they don't know something, hesitate to ask questions, or do not know what questions to ask.

For example, Steve W.'s first job out of college was as a customer service supervisor. "I was afraid to ask about certain things, like 'What is the company's policy on taking back merchandise that is damaged?' The people I supervise and my boss assume I know that, and I don't want to look like I'm incompetent."

Katherine G., on the other hand, a newly hired assistant to an account executive of a large public relations firm, felt that she was always running to her boss to ask questions. "I prefer to work more independently," she said. "I would feel more comfortable looking things up in a manual or handbook if we had one."

Where to Focus

Orientation should concentrate on issues unique to the employee's immediate workplace and job, including the physi-

Orientation should concentrate on issues unique to the employee's immediate workplace and job, including the physical environment; expectations; rules and regulations; fringe benefits; and focused, results-oriented, on-the-job training.

cal environment; expectations; rules and regulations; fringe benefits; and focused, results-oriented, on-the-job training. Later on—from three to six months after the employee is hired—orientation should provide a working understanding of your business and an in-depth exposure to corporate functions, how deparetments interrelate, and where the new employee fits. Many of these employees have not made definite or final decisions about their career paths; a detailed orientation to various departments over a period of months can help with that decision.

For example, TechAge, a 24,000-employee computer graphics firm, offers a one-day orientation session entitled "Perspectives" to entry-level professionals and others who have been with the company for one year. The purpose of "Perspectives" is to resell new employees on the company and to reinforce their decision to join it. The program begins with a presentation by the company president of the overall purpose, objectives, and management structure of the company so as to give participants an understanding of what the business is all about. The president then fields questions from the participants. The program later discusses how to get ahead in the company and provides a more detailed look at benefits like stock options and profit sharing and their implications for employees.

TRAINED AND EXPERIENCED NEW EMPLOYEES

Often referred to as "older workers" (age 40 and above), these employees have a strong sense of themselves and are eager to show what they can do. They are concerned about making it in the new environment and want recognition for their skills and achievements. They need a friendly, supportive environment and the opportunity to apply what they have learned and to build new learning on past experiences.

Experienced employees may bring along habits and attitudes that conflict with the company message. For example, recessionary pressures have forced many experienced individuals who have been in business for themselves to "go captive" and seek full-time employment. These new employees may initially resist working within a more structured environment and attempt to exercise a work style that is inconsistent with that structure.

Sometimes unspoken assumptions come into play between the new employee and supervisor. For example, the supervisor may assume that "he knows what he's doing, he has lots of experience" or that "she'll pick it up as she goes along" and not spend much time introducing the new, experienced employee to the work environment. The employee may interpret this lack of attention to mean either that he or she has carte blanche to determine the job priorities or that "management just doesn't care."

Where to Focus

Employees with prior experience have a longer learning curve and need more time to become acclimated to their new work environment. You should tap the insights and ideas of experienced employees by grouping them together in the general orientation sessions and using them to teach others. The best approach for departmental orientation is self-paced learning, with short segments of material that break information down into digestible pieces. This group of employees tends to find credibility in the printed word; thus, most of them benefit from seeing any orientation information in print.

EXECUTIVES AND OTHER HIGHLY EXPERIENCED NEW EMPLOYEES

Effective orientation is most critical for highly experienced employees—executives transferring from another company, sector, division, or industry. These employees are most inclined to make assumptions about the organization, the

> Everyone has an invisible sign hanging from his neck saying Make Me Feel Important! Never forget this message when working with people.
>
> —MARY KAY ASH

> **If our people develop faster than a competitor's people, then they're worth more.**
>
> —**JOHN M. BIGGAR**

people, and company strengths and weaknesses, goals, culture, climate, and so forth. They are most concerned with the nature of the business, company goals, and various functions and levels of responsibility.

Where to Focus

Orientation for executives requires individualized programs customized to the needs of each individual, taking into consideration that person's background and job function. Often senior executives choose to attend the regular new employee orientation sessions so that they can get a thorough grounding in the details of the business and become better acquainted with the types of employees that make up the organization.

DISADVANTAGED EMPLOYEES

Impoverished living conditions, poor schooling, poor employment history, and perhaps even a police record are what the disadvantaged employee brings to the workplace. Maintaining reasonable productivity levels with this group is a major challenge because disadvantaged employees often lack the technical, communication, and analytical skills required of most jobs. Disadvantaged employees need lots of counseling and encouragement in the most basic activities, since few of their life experiences have provided them with the incentive to succeed.

Where to Focus

Orientation programs should deal with the most basic workplace standards—hygiene, dress, punctuality, attendance, the person to call if they are going to be absent, and so on. In regions where the labor pool is small, some companies, especially those in the service sector, teach basic reading, writing, and communication skills.

DISABLED EMPLOYEES

The passage of the Americans with Disabilities Act in 1990 has brought to the forefront a pool of willing and able, and often hitherto untapped, workers. People with disabilities want to become as much a part of the corporate mainstream as nondisabled employees are.

Where to Focus

The primary concern in orienting people with disabilities is to remove the effect of the disability by making appropriate accommodations. For deaf employees, sign-language interpreters can communicate appropriate information, video presentations can be closed-captioned, or information can be written so that deaf employees can rely more on their sense of sight. Supported employment programs are a special type of on-the-job training in which job coaches work one-on-one with mentally retarded persons. For blind persons, your program can be adapted by using audio presentations, written materials in braille, or live readers.

You also need to consider potential architectural barriers for wheelchair users or people with missing limbs. For example, when a quadriplegic applied for a position as financial consultant at a brokerage firm, the human resources representative sat down with him individually and provided him with a general orientation instead of the regular group orientation session, which, because of its location, would have placed a hardship on the new employee.

EMPLOYEES WHOSE SECOND LANGUAGE IS ENGLISH

A shortage of entry-level workers and professionals with esoteric or highly technical skills has forced many companies to hire recent immigrants whose English-language skills are not fully developed.

> Employees are not only members of the organization which employs them, they are also members of our society, other organizations, unions, consumer groups, and so on. From these various other roles they bring with them demands, expectations, and cultural norms . . .
>
> —EDGAR H. SCHEIN

Where to Focus

Presentations should be primarily visual, concentrating on "showing" rather than "telling." Interpreters can be used to convey more vital information. Participants who understand English can also help you to communicate the main ideas to others. Written materials can be translated into other languages. If your employee group is more highly skilled, reinforce the importance of knowing English as a requisite to getting ahead.

PART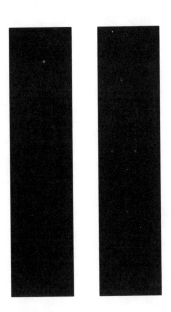

DESIGNING AND CONDUCTING YOUR PROGRAM

CHAPTER 4

DESIGNING YOUR ORIENTATION PROGRAM

When you have pinpointed where your company's new employee orientation efforts should focus, you have completed the important preliminaries to the design of your program. Now you need to consider:

- What topics or areas should the orientation session cover?
- Which parts of the orientation session should be presented orally and which through written materials?
- What audiovisuals will be used to communicate the message?
- How will the program be publicized?
- Who will deliver the orientation sessions?

The chief aim of the general orientation is to make new employees feel welcome and proud to be a part of your company.

The orientation program covers two types of information: that which is general to all employees, and that which is unique to each new employee. The first is covered in a general orientation conducted by the human resources representative or the designated coordinator; the second is conducted by the line manager or supervisor.

GENERAL ORIENTATION

The chief aim of the general orientation is to make new employees feel welcome and proud to be a part of your company. You must avoid overloading them with too much information at one time.

You can accomplish this with oral discussions of important information, augmented by audiovisuals. Written materials can also help parcel out information so that new employees can more readily absorb it over the course of several days or weeks.

You should include the following features in your program:

1. *An introduction to who and what the company is, where it has been, and where it is going.* New employees can more easily grasp the essence of what your company is all about when the president or another top executive in person gives a brief overview of the company during the program. Annual reports, sections in the employee handbook, or slide presentations help reinforce the senior executive's remarks.

2. *Highlights of important policies and practices.* You should discuss such policies as the introductory, or probationary, employment period; safety policies; performance standards; discipline and grievance procedures; and rules and regulations. You may wish to "walk" new employees through key points in the employee handbook or policy manual.

3. *The nature of the employer-employee relationship.* This means the company's expectations of employees concerning teamwork, attitude, loyalty, and quality of work; and what employees can expect from the company, such as salary increases, performance reviews, working conditions, recognition, opportunities for advancement, and fair treatment. As with policies and practices, you can "walk" new employees through any written materials that address these points.

4. *Your company's customer service philosophy, mission, and goals.* Employees need to know not only what customer service looks, sounds, and feels like but also in what ways they are responsible and held accountable for supporting the company's customer service strategies. In addition, you need to discuss customer service from the employee-as-customer perspective, focusing on the questions, "Would I buy the product I produce or use the service I provide?" Getting employees to view themselves as consumers of the compa-

ny's products or services encourages them to accept personal responsibility for customer service.

You have the option of covering the information listed below individually with each new employee prior to the first day of work, during the orientation program, or within a time period after the employee has begun work that does not exceed benefit enrollment or other deadlines.

5. *Review of benefits and services.* You should discuss not only the benefits themselves but also the cost, if any, to the employee and what percentage of payroll the company spends on employee benefits.

6. *Benefit plans enrollment.* You should assist employees in filling out the necessary forms and make sure that they understand the provisions and options of their benefits plans. If employees need time to discuss options with their spouses, they should be allowed to do so and informed of any enrollment deadlines.

7. *Miscellaneous employment documents.* You must see to it that identification cards, emergency notification forms, withholding information, and any other necessary forms are completed by new employees.

Orientations take many forms. Two different types are illustrated in the boxes on pages 32 and 33.

It is difficult for new employees to take in too much new information all at once. To avoid information overload, some companies opt for presenting their general orientation programs in two parts.

When deciding which parts of your program should be presented orally and which should be written, a good rule of thumb to follow is this: When your objective is to build enthusiasm and company spirit and pride, the most effective way to get your message across is orally. When your objective is to convey factual information, the information should

A MAJOR HOTEL COMPANY'S WEEKLY ORIENTATION SESSIONS FOR NEW EMPLOYEES

☐ Welcome and introduction: What it means to work in a hotel
☐ History and profile of the company (slide show)

- Early beginnings
- The company today
- The hotel division—number of hotels and locations, number of projected new openings

☐ The Sleep-Tite Hotel

- Date opened, number of rooms, number of employees
- Special features—the atrium, gift shops, restaurants, lounge, pool
- How the hotel is managed—executive committee members and their responsibilities, other managers, manager on duty
- Guest profile
- Special packages—Escape Weekends, conventions, family

☐ Benefits

- Insurance: life, medical, dental, optional disability
- Time off: sick days, vacation days, holidays, funeral leave, jury duty, leave of absence
- Your money: credit union, retirement, profit sharing, stock option, discounts
- Miscellaneous: tuition reimbursement, meals, uniforms

☐ Paydays
☐ Wage increase schedule
☐ Employee entrance/exit
☐ Dress standards
☐ Accident prevention and safety
☐ Parking
☐ Department meetings
☐ Lockers
☐ Rules and regulations
☐ Guarantee of fair treatment/progressive discipline
☐ Sleep-Tite Hotel employees in action (slide show)

be distributed to employees in writing so that they can digest it as needed.

At a bank in the Midwest, an "Employee's Personal Record" form is distributed to all new employees (see the box on

A MIDSIZE MANUFACTURING COMPANY'S TWO-PART GENERAL ORIENTATION FORMAT

Orientation Program Agenda
NBT Corporation

Part One (conducted on employees' first day of work and lasting approximately two hours)

☐ Introduction and welcome by the company president
☐ Discussion of company philosophy: "Our people are important"
☐ Overview of three key company employment principles:

1. Clear expectations on the part of employees of the job to be done and of the rewards for properly meeting expectations
2. Treating individuals with dignity and respect
3. Commitment to lifetime skills training and continued personal growth

☐ Discussion of general policies and procedures by human resources representative

- Vacation and sick leave
- Pay, raises, and promotions
- Rules of conduct

Introduction to new employees' managers and departmental orientation

Part Two (conducted one week later)

☐ Overview of and sign-up for benefits

- Medical insurance
- Dental insurance
- Life insurance
- Disability insurance

pages 34–38). Each point is covered by the human resources representative conducting the session. At its conclusion, each new employee signs the form; the human resources representative then collects one copy for inclusion in the employee's personnel file, while the employee retains the other copy as

(Text continues on page 38.)

HEARTLAND BANK
EMPLOYEE'S PERSONAL RECORD
OF ORIENTATION PROGRAM

1. Workweek and overtime. Heartland Bank's workweek is based on 40 hours and begins on _____ and ends on _____ . Overtime hours are all hours worked in excess of a 40-hour workweek. Overtime pay is at the rate of time and one-half for all hours worked over 40 hours each workweek, provided the employee is not exempt from overtime.

2. Time record. Each nonexempt employee is required to maintain an accurate record of the time worked. This record will be completed manually by each employee, and the following rules will be applied with regard to the record itself:

- No one else may record an individual's time.
- No pencil entries are allowed.
- The employee must sign the time card and give it to the supervisor.
- The supervisor must verify the hours, approve the time card, and submit it to the Human Resources Department by _____ , 19__ .

3. New employees progress report. All new employees are on a 90-day probationary period. During these first 90 days, your supervisor will review your performance at 30-day intervals, and this review will be discussed with you. Based on these reviews, a decision will be made as to whether or not it is in the best interests of both you and Heartland Bank to continue your employment before or at the conclusion of the 90 days.

4. Job description. Your supervisor will provide you with a copy of your job description as part of your departmental orientation. Please read it carefully. You are encouraged to ask questions about any of your job responsibilities, especially during your 90-day probationary period.

5. Labor unions. The management of Heartland has operated for more than 50 years on the basic philosophy of fairness in all its dealings with employees and customers. Heartland offers, and will continue to offer, good employee benefits, good working conditions, good hours, and salaries that are competitive for our industry. Unions have no responsibility to produce the profits required to provide salaries, benefits, buildings, equipment, and all other things necessary to keep a company in business. Since a union is not the employer, it can only get for its members what a company is willing to give. A company must have more interest in its employees than does a union. Business survival depends upon hiring, training, and promoting capable employees who can progress and assume greater responsibilities. Heartland has always dealt fairly and squarely with its employees. Proof of this statement is the fact that our employees have consistently rejected overtures from unions for many years.

6. Suggestions and complaints. We operate on the principle that most problems that are communicated can be solved. Procedures for making suggestions and complaints are outlined in your employee handbook, as well as in the personnel manual, which is available from your supervisor or the human resources department.

7. Code of conduct. The purpose of this code is to make employees aware of their legal and moral responsibility to Heartland Bank and it customers. Each employee is to read the Code of Conduct and complete the Statement of Compliance.

8. Apparent irregularities. You are requested and urged to report directly to _____ any apparent irregularities of any type that may come to your attention in the course of business. This information will be held in strict confidence.

9. Change in status. You are to notify your supervisor should you change your address, telephone number, exemptions, or marital status so that your personnel records can be kept up to date at all times.

(continues)

10. Termination. If you plan to terminate your employment for any reason, you are requested to notify your immediate supervisor and/or the human resources department at least two weeks before you leave.

11. Employee handbook. This handbook explains Heartland's policies, procedures, and benefits. You are asked to read this handbook as soon as possible and to jot down any questions you may have. Any changes that have been made since this edition was printed will be covered during today's session. Each of the policies in the handbook is further defined in either the personnel manual or the operations manual, both of which are available through your supervisor or human resources representative.

12. Training. The training department maintains books, records, tapes, and other materials relating to various phases of Heartland Bank's business, including training and supervision.

13. Job posting. Job posting provides the opportunity for employees to apply for nonexempt job openings prior to external recruitment of applicants and thereby reinforces Heartland's policy of promotion from within. (Probationary employees are not eligible to apply for posted positions.)

14. Savings and thrift plan. The savings and thrift plan encourages employees to put away money earned today and invest it for the future. All employees are eligible to join the plan on January 1. Deductions are made every payday; statements reflecting all contributions and earnings will be issued in September and December.

15. Insurance. Heartland Bank has an excellent insurance program through Rainyday Insurance Company providing group life, disability, major medical, and dental benefits. The individual booklets describe each program. Coverage takes effect the day your application is signed, but no later than the thirty-first day of your employment.

16. Payday. Payday is every other Friday. Pay is automatically deposited into an employee checking account unless you select the option of receiving your pay by check. You will receive a statement of earnings and deductions each payday indicating the amount of your earnings, deductions, and net pay. Heartland Bank considers your salary confidential. Questions concerning pay or deductions should be asked of your immediate supervisor. If your supervisor cannot provide you with a clear explanation, the supervisor will call the human resources department for an explanation, or you and your supervisor may visit the human resources department to obtain an explanation.

17. Holidays. All Heartland Bank offices observe the following eight holidays: New Year's Day, Martin Luther King, Jr., Day, President's Day, Memorial Day, Independence Day, Labor Day, Thanksgiving Day, and Christmas Day.

18. Vacation. You will be eligible for vacation at Heartland Bank if you work at least 20 hours each week and satisfactorily complete your 90-day probationary period. Complete details are given in your employee handbook.

19. Illness and absence. If personal illness or any other reason prevents you from being at work, it is your responsibility to notify your immediate supervisor by the time you would normally report to work. Further details on the employee absence policy are listed in your employee handbook. Note: Frequent absences may result in termination of your employment.

20. Accidents at work or while on Heartland Bank Business. If you are injured at work or while on bank business, you are to report the injury immediately to your supervisor or to the human resources department.

21. Equal employment opportunity. Heartland Bank believes in equal employment opportunity for all without regard to race, color, age, religion, sex, or national origin. We want you to know this so that you can become better acquainted with Heartland Bank and its practices.

(continues)

> **22. Confidentiality.** Business conducted at Heartland Bank is strictly confidential and information should never be discussed or disclosed to other persons except insofar as it is necessary in the regular course of business.
>
> Signature _____ Date: _____

a reference and reinforcement of the information that has been covered in the session.

DEPARTMENTAL ORIENTATION

The supervisor is the key person to get new employees over the "new job jitters" and to help them understand the new job and its relationship to the rest of the operation and the organization.

The key to all business management lies in the words: directing human activities.

—J. Paul Getty

The departmental orientation is the ideal time for the supervisor to begin building rapport with new employees. The departmental orientation provides information that is unique to each new employee's job and workplace and should be conducted by the supervisor immediately after the new employee has participated in a general orientation. The key elements of a departmental orientation include:

1. *Introduction to co-workers and others with whom the employee will have frequent on-the-job contact.* To allow the new employee to match names with faces, the supervisor should introduce people a few at a time. The supervisor should assign someone to be the new employee's mentor to continue the introductions and to take him or her to breaks and lunch.

2. *Tour of the department and surrounding facilities.* On the first day, the employee should be introduced to his or her immediate work area, and then, on subsequent days, to the other facilities until all facilities are covered.

3. *Introduction to the job.* The supervisor should have

work assignments ready for the employee on the first day so that he or she is immediately involved and productive.

The supervisor should review and complete with the new employee a departmental orientation checklist. On the second day of work, the supervisor should sit down with the new employee and answer any questions that may have come up after the first day on the job.

In the boxes on pages 40–44, you will find a variety of checklists for the manager or supervisor to cover with new employees.

SELECTING AUDIOVISUALS

Your primary considerations in selecting audiovisuals are which ones are best for reaching the people in your organization and how much money you are willing to spend. The most common audiovisuals used in orientation programs are videos, chalkboards, charts, posters, flipcharts, audios, slides, and overhead transparencies.

Videos can be used in place of live demonstrations and appearances. For example, if the CEO or other top official is located at another site, or is unable to be physically present at the orientation session each time, a "message from the President" can be videotaped and replayed at each session.

Not only is there an art in knowing a thing, but also a certain art in teaching it.

—CICERO

However, videos are costly unless you have substantial in-house capabilities. At commercial rates, professional-quality video production costs from $2,000 to $5,000 per minute. Furthermore, new developments and technological innovations quickly render the information obsolete, requiring you to constantly change them.

In addition to the actual production of the video, there is an investment in the playback units and monitors required. If you plan to use the video at multiple sites, you must consider the cost of mass-producing and distributing multiple copies as well.

If you choose to produce a video, you need to decide if you want your video to be accompanied by a scripted audio

DEPARTMENT ORIENTATION CHECKLIST

Department Manager: Please complete and return to Human Resources for retention in employee's file.

Employee name: _____

Department: _____ Job title: _____

Hire date: _____ Orientation date: _____

General Rules

☐ Welcome to department
☐ Personal appearance and cleanliness
☐ Smoking
☐ Injuries/first aid/reporting injuries
☐ Personal phone calls/visitors
☐ No return after work/no loitering
☐ Customer relations
☐ Locker assignment

Policies

☐ Locker room inspection
☐ Parking
☐ Removing items from premises
☐ Meals
☐ Clothing
☐ Hiring
☐ Call in
☐ Accident prevention
☐ Probationary period
☐ Grievance procedures

Departmental Specifics

☐ Telephone number
☐ Job description and responsibilities

☐ Explanation of schedule:
- hours of work
- lunch periods
- break times, smoking areas

☐ Location of time clock
☐ Location of rest rooms
☐ Attendance requirements
- absenteeism
- punctuality
- medical release/sick slip

☐ Responsibility to other departments
☐ Responsibility to co-workers
☐ Lines of authority
☐ Job training
☐ Safety training
- Location of stairwells and fire exits
- Location of fire extinguishers
- Special hazards

☐ Department tour
☐ Department introductions
☐ Assign mentor

Manager's signature: _____ Date: _____

Employee's signature: _____ Date: _____

narrative, written either in-house or by an outside script-writer. If you use an outside scriptwriter, be sure it is someone who is familiar with your industry so that the script does not sound canned or unrealistic.

Chalkboards are inexpensive and require no special technical skills, but materials have to be rewritten each time they are presented and then erased. *Posters and charts,* on the other hand, can be used over and over again and are most effective when kept simple. Written messages should be limited to one or two sentences or no more than four short points.

Flipcharts are useful for jotting down key points as they come up, but can also be prepared ahead of time. They are a more

(Text continues on page 44.)

NEW MANAGER'S ORIENTATION CHECKLIST

Please complete and return to Human Resources for retention in employee's file.

Manager's name: _____

Department: _____

Department head: _____

- ☐ Company and department tour
- ☐ Visit with executive vice-president
- ☐ Visit with president
- ☐ Visit with human resources director
  - Receive manager's handbook.
  - Enroll in benefits.
  - Review schedule for appropriate new manager training programs.
  - Review wage scale for manager's department.
- ☐ Visit with controller
  - Review expense account policies.
- ☐ Nonmanagement orientation session (within first week)

Manager's signature:

_____ Date: _____

Department head's signature:

_____ Date: _____

Human resources director's signature:

_____ Date: _____

PROFESSIONAL/TECHNICAL EMPLOYEE ORIENTATION CHECKLIST

☐ Provide employee with job description for position.

☐ Explain specific requirements and expected accomplishments.

☐ Provide overview of the organization and mission of the department, its relationship to other departments, and the employee's role as it relates to the goals of the department.

☐ Introduce employee to department staff.

☐ Provide tour of facility and introduce employee to employees outside of the department.

☐ Review:
- Working hours
- Lunch period
- Jury duty
- Overtime
- Probation period
- Illnesses
- Military obligation
- Time and attendance reporting
- Personal emergencies
- Performance appraisals

☐ Review benefits:
- Insurance (life, disability, medical, travel accident, workers' compensation)
- Tuition reimbursement
- Holidays
- Sick days
- Vacation days
- Career development
- Employee assistance program

☐ Review paperwork for completeness:
- Application
- Signature on employment agreement
- Personnel questionnaire
- I.D. card
- W-4 form
- Sales forms
- Insurance applications

(continues)

☐ Provide employee with:
- Employee handbook
- "Where to Go" guide
- Time card
- Security procedures
- Copy of newsletter
- Building layout
- Organization chart
- History and product line
- Telephone directory
- Restaurant guide

☐ Make public announcement on bulletin board of new employee's name, position, and starting date.

personal method of presentation than video and can be used to elicit participation from the audience.

Slides are compact and easy to manage, and they render clearly detailed images if the photography is of high quality. Message content can be updated by replacing individual slides with new ones. Additional or replacement slides can be easily inserted at the desired sequence in the program. The individual conducting the orientation can discuss details with the participants while showing each slide, or an audio script can accompany the slides.

Overhead transparencies, like chalkboards and flipcharts, are inexpensive, easy to prepare, and require no special technical expertise to use. They are a good way to show organization charts, cartoons, or caricatures illustrating points to be made in the orientation program, and company mission statements, operating philosophy statements, slogans, and other simple messages.

Use the questions below to help you select what type, style, and number of audiovisuals your program requires:

How many participants will be in each orientation session?

_____

_____

_____

_____

What levels of employees (e.g., middle management, production and line workers) will be attending?

_____

_____

_____

_____

Which types of audiovisuals will get the message across most effectively to the greatest number of participants?

_____

_____

_____

_____

At how many locations will we be conducting orientation sessions?

_____

_____

_____

_____

Will we need to have more than one set of audiovisuals to distribute to multiple sites?

_____

_____

_____

_____

What can we afford to spend producing audiovisuals?

_____

_____

_____

_____

What vendors should we use? (What experience have they had with producing orientation audiovisuals? Which ones have a good understanding of our industry?)

_____

_____

_____

_____

Which audiovisuals can be adapted to the needs of disabled participants?

_____

_____

_____

_____

How easily can we update audiovisual materials?

_____

_____

PUBLICIZING YOUR PROGRAM

Ensuring adequate participation is an important part of your program design. Here are some suggested methods for getting the word out:

1. Indicate the time and place on an employee confirmation form or letter (as in the boxes on pages 48–52).
2. Send a personal invitation to the employee's home, with a copy to the immediate supervisor or department head.
3. Send a memorandum to the immediate supervisor or department head indicating the date, time, place, and participants.
4. Place large, colorful posters in strategic places such as break rooms and cafeterias or on bulletin boards to announce the date, time, and location of the orientation.
5. Announce the orientation in your company newsletter; highlight the announcement with boxes or other graphics.

And if you really want to go all out, consider some of these aggressive ideas. At a large travel services company, a staff member, dressed up as a well-known cartoon character, distributed flyers in the lobby announcing the orientation program. An overview video ran in the cafeteria at lunchtime, and copies of literature used in the orientation were placed on a table next to the video. Meetings were held with managers to provide them with an overview, and management guides to orientation were distributed. One week

CONFIRMATION OF EMPLOYMENT FORM

To: _____ Date: _____

From: _____

Human resources representative

_____

CONFIRMATION

Position: _____

Department: _____ Unit: _____

Department head: _____

Supervisor: _____

_____

REPORT DATES

Physical exam: _____ Work: _____

Orientation: _____

_____

BASIC SALARY DATA

Starting salary: _____ per _____

Salary differential: _____ per _____

Hours of work: _____ A.M./P.M. to _____ A.M./P.M.

Total hours per week: ____ ☐ Paid weekly ☐ Biweekly

Probationary period: _____ to _____

beginning date   ending date

Next increase/review date: _____

_____

EMPLOYMENT CLASSIFICATION

☐ Full-time   ☐ Regular   ☐ Exempt
☐ Part-time   ☐ Contingent   ☐ Nonexempt

APPROVALS

_____   _____
Employee   Human resources
                                 representative

_____
Department head

---

before the orientation was to be held, managers were called by the Human Resources Department and asked if they needed any help or advice before the program. Articles appeared in the company newsletter. A wallet card with "Nine Excellent Employee Practices" detailed on one side and important telephone numbers printed on the reverse side were distributed. Posters of each of the "Nine Excellent Employee Practices" were made and displayed in both the reception area and employee work areas.

Written confirmations of employment and orientation are important to make sure new employees show up for the session. They serve as reminders to new employees and provide a reassuring direction to employees who may be anxious about the first day of work.

GIVING YOUR PROGRAM VERSATILITY

Your orientation program should aim for consistency of information and flexibility in the ways that information is conveyed. You should be able to tailor your program to different circumstances from one part of the company to the

---

SIMPLE CONFIRMATION OF EMPLOYMENT LETTER

[Date]

Dear _____:

It is my pleasure to welcome you to _____, and we are delighted that you have accepted the position of _____. As we discussed, your starting date is _____ and your starting salary will be _____ per _____.

We have scheduled you to attend our new employee orientation session on _____ at _____ A.M., in _____. You will be introduced to the company, find out what you can expect from us and what we expect from you, and learn about opportunities for growth and development that exist with us.

We are confident that you will be a great addition to our team, and we look forward to working with you.

Sincerely,

_____

Human resources representative

cc: *[Department Manager/Supervisor]*

---

other and to different work groups. Here are some ways in which to add versatility to your program:

1. Create a literature kit to keep employees informed about work-related news, trends, and other relevant company information. A pharmaceutical company includes its mission statement, business goals and objectives, and an employee benefits summary on 8½ × 11 laminated sheets. (See the two boxes on pages 53 and 54.)

DETAILED CONFIRMATION OF EMPLOYMENT LETTER

W * E * L * C * O * M * E

[*Date*]

Dear _____:

We welcome you to Jiffy Corporation, and we welcome your help in getting the job done!

Here is some basic information you will need to know before you get started on _____.

Your department: _____ Title: _____ Clock No.: _____

Your supervisor's name: _____

Telephone: Call _____, ext. _____, if you are out sick or will be late.

Your hours of work: _____ to _____.

Your lunch period: _____ to _____, except on _____, which is payday, when the lunch period is from _____ to _____ to allow you more time to go to the bank.

Payday: Paychecks are distributed before lunch on _____.

Probation: Your probation period ends on _____.

Insurance: Your insurance becomes effective on _____.

Sick days: You are entitled to _____ sick days per year. Your sick day accruals begin on _____.

(continues)

Performance review: Your first performance review will be on _____.

Holidays: Regular company holidays observed at Jiffy are New Year's Day, Martin Luther King, Jr., Day, President's Day, Memorial Day, Independence Day, Labor Day, Thanksgiving Day, Christmas Eve, and Christmas Day.

Vacation: You are entitled to two weeks' vacation per year. Your vacation credit accruals begin _____.

Breaks: You are entitled to two breaks per day, one in the morning and one in the afternoon. Check with your supervisor as to what time your department takes breaks.

Special conditions of employment:

You will learn more about Jiffy and the particulars of your position at an orientation program scheduled for _____.

We look forward to having you as part of our team! Sincerely,

_____
Human resources representative

Key materials you could include in the literature kit you create are:

- Employee handbook
- In-house newsletters
- Companywide publications
- Safety information
- Benefits enrollment forms
- Employee's job description
- Special announcements
- Relevant business and industry articles
- Name tags (if used)
- Job information questionnaire regarding key aspects

LIFELINE PHARMACEUTICAL COMPANY STRATEGIC FRAMEWORK

Mission	Goals	Objectives
	People	
• We are a worldwide team committed to creating distinctive solutions for the needs of mankind in pharmaceutical and consumer health products. • We measure our success by the achievement of market leadership, superior financial returns, and an environment of trust and personal growth. • We accomplish this through the dedication of all of us and all of our resources to continuous improvement in all that we do.	• Develop and maintain a team of motivated and talented individuals working in an environment that fosters accomplishment, creativity, mutual respect, and the opportunity for each person to realize his or her full potential.	• Establish a common understanding of organizational structure, responsibility, accountability, and authority by 12/92 • Achieve improvement in productivity (+20% sales and +40% profit per employee) by 1993 • Ensure that we are a company driven by a defined set of shared values • Establish reward and appraisal system based on performance

Strategies

• Define and communicate company values to all employees on an ongoing basis
• Establish comprehensive orientation and training programs for all units

of the job to be signed and dated by the new employee (see box on pages 55–57)

New employees tend to be anxious during the first few days of a new job. To prevent any misunderstanding, include this statement with the questionnaire: "My signature indicates that the above items have been explained to me and that I understand everything." Emphasize to new employees that they should *not* sign a checklist unless they are sure they understand everything that has been outlined to them.

(Text continues on page 57.)

A SUMMARY OF LIFELINE PHARMACEUTICAL COMPANY EMPLOYEE BENEFITS

Benefit	Who Is Eligible	When Eligible	What You Receive
Medical plan	Full-time employees	Immediately	Necessary medical care, accident treatment, surgery, and other miscellaneous covered expenses, up to $1 million in lifetime major medical coverage
Dental plan	Full-time employees	Immediately	Coverage for routine and special treatment
Life insurance	Full-time employees	Immediately	Coverage of one to four times base annually; spouse coverage also available
Short-term disability	Full-time employees	Immediately	Financial benefits if unable to perform regular job duties
Holidays	Full- and part-time employees	After 90 days	9 paid regular holidays and birthday
Sick leave	Full- and part-time employees	After 90 days	10 days annually
Vacation	Full- and part-time employees	After 1 year	2 weeks
Jury duty	Full-time employees	Immediately	Paid absence
Leave of absence	All employees	After 6 months	For medical or approved personal reasons
Profit sharing	All employees	After 1 year	Share in company profits

JOB INFORMATION QUESTIONNAIRE

Name: _____   Date of employment: _____

Department: _____   Position: _____

Complete the questionnaire as well as you can. Then take it to your supervisor, who will go over it with you and give you any additional information you need.

You are expected to return this questionnaire, signed by your department head, to the Human Resources Department three weeks after your date of employment.

If for any reason you cannot keep the appointment below, have your department head schedule you for another time.

Appointment date and time: _____

Place: Human Resources Department

Department head signature: _____ Date: _____

1. The job of my department is _____.

2. The most important part of my job is _____.

3. My department head's name is _____, my supervisor's name is _____.

4. I receive my time card from _____.

5. Time cards must be turned in on _____ to

day
    _____. Payday is _____.

person

6. If I feel ill at work, I should _____.

(continues)

7. If I feel ill at home, I should notify my supervisor by calling _____ at least _____

telephone number   number of minutes

before I am expected at work.

8. My work hours are _____.

9. Any changes in my work schedule are arranged by _____.

10. Work assignments are given to me by _____.

11. I can get help from _____.

12. Some of my job duties include:

   _____

   _____

   _____

   _____

13. In doing my work I handle the following:
   ☐ paper   ☐ equipment   ☐ supplies
   ☐ food   ☐ products   ☐ customers

14. If I use equipment, I use _____. To keep equipment in good working order, I must _____.

15. If I work with supplies, products, or food, the way I handle them is important because _____ _____.

16. If I work with customers, my work is important because _____ _____.

17. To keep things running smoothly, I should bring to the attention of my supervisor the following: ____ _____.

18. My performance on the job will be measured by
    _____.

19. Two safety rules that apply to my job are: _____
    _____.

20. Two company rules that particularly apply to my
    job are:
    _____.

21. I have had the most difficulty with the following
    on my job:
    _____.

22. Things I'd like to know more about are _____
    _____.

23. Things I like best about my job are _____
    _____.

24. Suggestions: _____
    _____
    _____
    _____

2. Create an employee orientation calendar so that new employees know what they are expected to accomplish during the orientation process (see box on page 58).

Alternatively, the orientation schedule could be incorporated in a letter to the new employee (see box on pages 59–60).

3. Use audiovisuals or interactive and noninteractive disks to create self-directed or self-study learning programs. Complete presentations can be placed on audiovisual equipment and on computer diskettes, which allows the program to be viewed at the convenience of the person conducting the orientation and of the new employee, outside of a formal

(Text continues on page 60.)

NEW EMPLOYEE ORIENTATION SCHEDULE
GOTHAM CORPORATION

Orientation schedule for: _____
employee's name

Position: _____   Dept: _____

Scheduled to report on: _____

Assignment	Date to be completed
Attend general orientation	3/12/9__
Attend benefits orientation	3/19/9__
Departmental orientation with manager	3/26/9__
Follow-up appointment with human resources representative	4/12/9__
Attend following sessions: "Attitudes: Dealing with Our Customers"	5/12/9__
"Growing with Gotham"	6/15/9__
"Teamwork: Our Key Ingredient"	7/20/9__
Appointment with human resources representative to review future training	8/1/9__

Signature: _____
Human resources representative

Date: _____

ORIENTATION SCHEDULE INCORPORATED IN LETTER

Dear _____ :

Welcome to _____ Corporation! We want your first 90 days with us to be exciting and productive. So that you can make the most of these first critical months, we are outlining an orientation program for you. Under the direction of your supervisor and the Human Resources Department, you are expected to participate in the following orientation activities over the next 90 days:

First day of work: August 15

9:00 A.M.–12:00 P.M.	Briefing with human resources representative: overview of organization, benefits, pay; completion of enrollment forms
12:00 P.M.–1:15 P.M.	Lunch with human resources representative
1:15P.M.–3:30 P.M.	Meet with department supervisor: review supervisor checklist form
3:30 P.M.–4:30 P.M.	Tour of different departments

Second day of work: August 16

9:00 A.M.–5:00 P.M.	Report to department as per regular schedule and receive work assignment; review performance goals and expectations with supervisor

(continues)

August 30

9:00 A.M.–12:00 noon   Formal orientation session in Executive Conference Room

September 16

10:00 A.M.–11:00 A.M.   Meeting with human resources representative for progress update and answers to questions that have arisen

November 14

10:00 A.M.–11:00 A.M.   Meeting with human resources representative and preparation for performance review/review of probationary status

November 15

Time to be decided   Performance reviews with supervisor

We are pleased that you have joined us. Please feel free to contact the human resources department or your supervisor whenever you have questions.

Sincerely,

_____

Human resources representative

class. This can be useful when the orientation requires a more tailored approach, as with the more experienced employee or executive. For the younger employee or the employee new to the work force, it is important that audiovisuals not be used as substitutes for interaction with supervisors or managers.

SELECTING PRESENTERS

The size of your company and the scope of your orientation process determine whether the coordinator of the orientation program conducts all of the general orientation sessions or whether session leaders should be selected and trained.

When choosing session leaders, make sure they possess the following characteristics:

- Experience in and enthusiasm for their respective areas of responsibility
- Ability to convey an understanding of the materials
- Empathy for and ability to reduce new employees' anxieties
- Demonstrated skills at organizing tasks and time

At Corning International's district office, supervisors learn in a three-hour workshop the orientation process, its rationale, and their roles. Orientation session leaders at individual plants include plant managers, the personnel manager, the controller, the engineering manager, the training coordinator, the production superintendent, and senior salespeople.

CHAPTER 5

CONDUCTING YOUR PROGRAM

When, in what way, and for how long you conduct your orientation program are affected by a variety of factors. What is most important is that new employees be introduced to the company, their jobs, their supervisors, and their co-workers and that they have a basic understanding of the benefits, rights, responsibilities, and mutual expectations on the first day or within the first week of employment.

For most companies, a general orientation is held for new employees on their first day of work. The new employees meet in a conference or training room. They are greeted by the person conducting the session, usually the human resources representative. Some companies provide soda, coffee, cookies, or other refreshments. The presenter gives an overview of the meeting, which typically follows an outline like the one below:

- The organization
  —History
  —Function
  —Organization chart
  —Culture and mission
- Discussion of company's products and services, marketplace position, and competition
- Industry jargon
- Organizational policies, rules and regulations, discipline and grievance procedures, attitude, attendance and punctuality requirements, dress standards, maintenance of company property

**Team spirit
is what
gives so
many com-
panies an
edge over
their com-
petitors.**

—GEORGE L.
CLEMENTS

- Compensation and benefits
  —Insurance
  —Time off
  —Pay policies
  —Vacation
  —Holidays
  —Overtime compensation
  —Performance review schedule
  —Pension and profit sharing programs
- Work schedules and work rules
- Safety and emergency procedures
- Employee recognition programs, attendance awards, suggestion system
- Generic job skills relating to basic information giving, customer relations, techniques for effective communication with co-workers, stress management
- Training opportunities

Try to add life and interest to your orientation session with a presentation that mixes both ad-libbed and scripted elements. In the box on pages 64–66 is the orientation script, used along with slides, of the Sleep-Tite Hotel Chain.

A copy of the employee handbook should be distributed to each person, and employees should be instructed to keep it at their workstations. The presenter should briefly review the contents and discuss questions with the group. Key company policies and the reasons for them should be emphasized. The representative should emphasize the importance of knowing the information in the handbook and point out its value as a reference tool for clarifying and reinforcing company policies.

The room in which you conduct your program may be set up "schoolroom" style, that is, with rows of tables in depth and a lectern at the front of the room. This room arrangement is an efficient way to get information across to both small and large groups, especially when time is limited.

(Text continues on page 66.)

ORIENTATION SCRIPT WITH SLIDE PRESENTATION

Welcome to the Sleep-Tite Hotel! Orientation Script With Slide Presentation [*slide*] Like most new employees, you may be feeling somewhat lost among unfamiliar faces and working conditions. This orientation program is designed to make you feel less new and more a part of the team. You will be given a lot of information in a short time.

We'll tell you how Sleep-Tite began, talk about the hotel division and this particular hotel, and show you real people in action. We don't promise that you will be an instant "old hand"—that takes time and experience—but you should walk away with a better understanding of what Sleep-Tite is all about.

First, let's go back to February 6, 1923, the date of what was to become the beginning of the Sleep-Tite Hotel Corporation. [*slide*] On that date, J. R. Higgins opened a boarding house in a small town just outside Dallas, Texas. [*slide*] Two years later, Mr. Higgins was operating the boarding house and three small hotels in Dallas and planning more, despite the Great Depression. [*slide*] By the end of World War II, there were nearly twenty hotels, at that time called the Higgins Inns.

During this growth period, Mr. Higgins decided on a different direction for his hotels. He wanted a name that more clearly expressed what his hotels offered to guests, and he wanted to create a name recognition. In 1957, the first Sleep-Tite Hotel [*slide*] was opened in Chicago and marked the entrance into a new market that spread across the country. [*slide*] By 1970 there were fifty Sleep-Tite Hotels in major cities in the United States. In 1975, Sleep-Tite entered the European market [*slide*] and opened a hotel in London. There are now ten hotels across Western

Europe [*slide*], with five hotels scheduled to open in Eastern Europe over the next two years.

Let's talk more about the hotel of which *you* are a part. [*slide*]

This hotel opened in January 1981. We are a medium-size hotel with 450 guest rooms, meeting rooms, and a 10,000-square-foot ballroom [*slide*] that can be broken down into smaller meeting rooms. The hotel restaurant [*slide*], Alice's, offers a relaxing, yet elegant, atmosphere for dining. The Lizard Lounge [*slide*] allows guests the opportunity to unwind and enjoy upbeat recorded music, and features as well a variety of activities like Monday night football or [*slide*] a Halloween costume contest. We also offer an indoor/outdoor pool and hot tub [*slide*], where guests can relax and eat or drink poolside.

To attract and keep our guests, we offer a number of special deals. Pearl Club [*slide*] is a service for repeat guests, which entitles them to express check-in service, a room on the Pearl floor, and a number of other special considerations. A holder of a Lizard Lounge Preferred Guest Card [*slide*] receives a 10 percent discount in the lounge. Escape Weekends [*slide*] provide reduced room rates, with meals included, for guests who want to take a brief vacation without leaving home.

Because of these features and our airport location [*slide*], our guests are primarily airline personnel, businesspeople, and small groups that choose to convene here.

Every Sleep-Tite Hotel is managed in the same way, and this hotel is no exception. The executive committee [*slide*] is the top management team of the hotel and consists of the following individuals: [*slide*] George Stanton, general manager; [*slide*] Sheila Morton, director of food and beverages, who is responsible for the Lizard Lounge, Alice's Restaurant, and banquet

(continues)

and catering activities; [*slide*] Beverly Lee, director of marketing, who runs the sales team; [*slide*] Chuck Eldridge, resident manager, who is responsible for the front office, housekeeping, and the laundry; [*slide*] Rob Erickson, who monitors the income and expenses of the hotel's departments; [*slides*] Gary Steele, who keeps the hotels' physical plant operating; and [*slide*] Kathleen O'Grady, director of human resources, who interacts with the 350-plus employees responsible for keeping the hotel running.

It is to our employees that Sleep-Tite owes its success. Sleep-Tite has a simple philosophy: [*slide*] Take care of the employees who take care of the guests. And that has been demonstrated over and over each time ground is broken for a new hotel.

Later in the program, we will tell you just how Sleep-Tite takes care of its guests and why they return.

Again, welcome. We're glad you're with us!

[*slides—employees-in-action candids*]

Rooms arranged with round tables are an effective way to get employees acquainted with each other. Since new employees may be nervous or afraid on their first day of work, you should avoid putting new employees on the spot by soliciting audience participation in your session.

Some orientation sessions allow for question-and-answer segments depending on the size of the group and the amount of time allotted for the meeting.

An orientation meeting can have as few as one participant or as many as hundreds. In the latter case, coordinating and conducting the orientation sessions is a bit like running a small conference.

In the box on pages 67–69, note the innovative way in which Speedy Courier Service oriented 400 new employees at a one-day session when the company opened a new facility in Denver, Colorado.

SPEEDY COURIER SERVICE
NEW EMPLOYEE ORIENTATION
SATURDAY, JULY 10

8:30 A.M.   **Registration**—Employee Cafeteria

All new employees (call center staff, sales support representatives, customer service representatives, messengers/drivers/dispatchers, and call center/customer service supervisors) will be greeted by a receptionist and directed to their respective registration desks to sign in with their manager and receive orientation packets containing:

- The orientation session agenda
- A time card
- Benefits sign-up forms
- A safety checklist
- The conditions of employment
- A copy of *Top Speed* newsletter
- The employee handbook

Coffee and pastries will be set up in the cafeteria. Information aides wearing Speedy Courier jackets will be available throughout the area to provide directions and help with traffic flow.

9:00 A.M.   **General session**—Truck Garage

Agenda

Speedy Courier Service slide
    presentation
Welcome and introduction of President
    by the Executive Vice-President
Opening remarks and introduction of
    senior staff by the President
Overview of daily schedule
Adjournment to group sessions

Chairs, a podium with lectern, microphone, screen, slide projector, and audio equipment will be set up.

(continues)

10:00 A.M.   **Group sessions**—Executive Dining Room and Company Cafeteria

Group 1—Call center staff
Group 2—Sales support representatives
Group 3—Customer service representatives
Group 4—Messengers/drivers/ dispatchers
Group 5—Call center/customer service supervisors

Session Descriptions

Session A: "Customer First at Speedy"
                    Presenter: Joe Adams

The session will focus on the basic elements of customer service, with a 13-minute film illustrating customer contact situations.

Session B: Company Organization
                    Presenter: Mike Wolfe

A brief overview of the history and growth of Speedy Courier Service will be provided, along with a summary of how the company is organized and the responsibilities of individual departments.

Session C: Facility Tour   **Tour Guide:** Al Burton

Employees will be taken on short walking tours of the facility.

Session D: Safety   **Presenter:** Sally Griffin

The session will focus on an overview of the kind of accidents that occur in our business, their cause and prevention, our loss prevention structure and programs, and emergency procedures in the event of fire, power failures, or disastrous weather conditions.

Session E: Benefits   **Presenter:** Mary Brady

The session will review all benefits offered to employees and allow employees to complete their benefits applications.

Session F: Conditions of Employment
Presenter: Gary Joyner

The session will cover all company rules and regulations and grievance and discipline procedures, and also review employee handbooks.

Rotation Sequence

	Groups				
	1	2	3	4	5
10:00–10:30 A.M.	E	D	F	C	B
10:30–11:00 A.M.	E	D	F	*	C
11:00–11:30 A.M.	C	E	D	F	*
11:30A.M.–12:00 noon	*	E	D	F	A
12:00–12:30 P.M.	A	*	E	D	F
12:30–1:00 P.M.	B	C	E	D	F
1:00–1:30 P.M.	F	A	*	E	D
1:30–2:00 P.M.	F	B	A	E	D
2:00–2:30 P.M.	D	F	B	A	E
2:30–3:00 P.M.	D	F	C	B	E

At 3:00 P.M., all employees will be directed to departmental meetings with their managers.

*Lunch

Employee Orientation Staff Assignments

Orientation Coordinator
Assistant Orientation Coordinator
Registration Coordinator
Receptionist
Information Coordinator
Session Leaders and Assistant Session Leaders
Information Aides
Audiovisual and Room Setup Coordinator

CHAPTER 6

SOME ORIENTATION SCENARIOS

All new employees, whether hourly, salaried, exempt, or nonexempt, need a solid orientation. There will be differences based on the new employee's position or level of job, but the basic program should provide a smooth transition to the new work environment for everyone.

The following action steps will ensure that your orientation program helps new employees get the most out of their first day at work:

1. *Recognize that the time between the employee's acceptance of the job and the start date is part of orientation.* It is during this time that the new employee, once the dust has settled, begins to feel the mixed emotions of excitement and anxiety. It is important to maintain contact with new employees through letters confirming employment and welcoming letters or phone calls.

2. *Model the initial impression you want to create for new employees.* If you want new employees to perceive that your company is people-oriented and fosters open communications, your words and actions should reflect this. If your company values a crisp appearance and professional demeanor, you and others with whom new employees will have initial contact should dress and act the part.

3. *Confine the focus of first-day activities and information to what new employees* need *to know.* Discuss working hours, lunch hours and breaks, and safety considerations, and give a brief overview of what to expect in the days or weeks to come.

4. *Explain key company policies or procedures that will help new employees to avoid making embarrassing mistakes.* These policies concern attendance and punctuality, parking spaces authorized for their use, office protocol, and so on.

5. *Avoid confusing new employees with too many names and faces.* Instead, select a small number of people new employees should meet initially, then gradually introduce them to others as appropriate.

6. *Be sure that new employees' workplaces are organized, physically comfortable, secure, and prepared for their arrival.* For example, the newcomer's office should be clean and stocked with appropriate supplies. Work areas of production workers should have the necessary tools at hand to do the job.

7. *Assign job-related tasks the first day so that new employees can immediately get into the rhythm of the job and the company.* Assignments should provide positive experiences so that new employees feel from the start that they have made a valuable contribution.

8. *Be available to new employees on their first day.* Provide personal attention that shows you care about their success.

The remainder of this chapter consists of a variety of scenarios illustrating how an orientation program is shaped by the type of company and the level of employee involved.

Choice Papers

John Evans had just received a verbal commitment from the area sales manager that he had been hired as a sales representative at Choice Papers, a 400-employee paper distributor. The sales manager walked him back to the human resources department and introduced him to the director of human resources, Ellen Shelby. Ms. Shelby scheduled an appointment with John for the Friday before his first day of work so that he could complete some of the employment paperwork. He was given a brochure with information on employee benefits and services, a W-2 form, background information on the company, and several product brochures to read prior to his appointment.

On the day of his appointment, Ms. Shelby met him in the reception area, offered him a cup of coffee, and showed him to the conference room, where the company vice-president awaited them. The vice-president welcomed John, spoke with him about the company philosophy and about opportunities at Choice Papers, and then left him with Ms. Shelby, who reviewed the benefits and services offered by the company. Although John already knew that Choice had a good benefits package, he was pleased to learn that it rivaled those offered by Fortune 500 corporations. Ms. Shelby made a note on her calendar to remind John to enroll in the group health plan no later than the thirtieth day of his employment.

When John arrived for his first day of work, the area sales manager greeted him, escorted him to his work area, and reviewed with him his job description, important and pertinent company policies relating to use of the company car, expense reports, and travel policies, and the performance appraisal procedure and format. The manager explained that for the first few weeks he would be working very closely with John in servicing accounts and accompanying him in the field. After approximately two hours, John clearly knew what was expected of him.

John's manager then took him on a tour of the immediate work area and showed John the work flow and where he fit in. He was introduced to others with whom he would be working. John and his manager continued their discussion of his work over lunch in the employee lunchroom, where he was introduced to employees of other departments.

After one month, John and his manager sat down, and John received a formal progress report. Since his manager had been working so closely with him, John knew on a daily basis where he stood; therefore, the formal progress report, which would go in his personnel file, contained no surprises. It was evident that John had become fully acclimated to his job and to the company and was ready to service accounts and go out into the field on his own.

After the formal progress report, John and his manager met weekly to continue reviewing his progress and to answer John's questions. One morning, as John was getting ready to leave to visit a customer, the president dropped by to congratulate him on his creditable performance over the past three months.

LL International

The more you learn about your job, the more you may earn from your job.

—NAPOLEAN HILL

LL International, a telecommunications firm with 375,000 employees in the United States and forty foreign countries, hired Ellen Becker as a word processing secretary for its corporate headquarters offices. When Ellen reported to work, she was directed to the conference room, where five other new employees, also word processing secretaries, met as a group in a three-hour session with personnel representatives. Coffee, soda, and pastries were available.

The meeting began at 9:00 A.M. with the employment manager, Robert Barnes, welcoming the new employees and outlining the agenda for the morning. The benefits representative provided an overview of the company's benefits and guided the new employees through the process of completing the paperwork. After collecting it, he turned the meeting back to Mr. Barnes.

Mr. Barnes proceeded to give an overview of the company, of how it was organized and how the word processing area serviced the departments, and then covered topics of immediate concern to new employees, such as pay, hours of work, and attendance. He next handed out a performance review form and discussed how performance was evaluated and what the comany expected from its employees. Mr. Barnes distributed a supervisor checklist, explained its purpose—to help supervisors remember specific items to be discussed during the departmental orientation—and instructed the new employees to give the checklist to their respective supervisors.

**The longer
you're in
a new job,
the more
you develop
a personal
sense of
comfort.**

—JOHN J.
GABARRO

He showed the new employees a recent company newsletter and indicated that it was only one of many ways the company used to keep employees informed about what was going on. Then the employment manager took the six new employees to lunch in the employee cafeteria (this first lunch was on the company), pointing out that lunch was a company benefit and informing them of the hours and costs.

After lunch, Mr. Barnes escorted them to their department and introduced them to their supervisor. Ellen and her co-workers spent the balance of the afternoon with their supervisor reviewing the supervisory checklist form (see box on this page) and being introduced to the work area and the other workers.

A tour of the work area and the building finished the day.

On the second day, the supervisor and Ellen sat down together to discuss performance expectations in more detail,

---

NEW EMPLOYEE CHECKLIST
WORD PROCESSING DEPARTMENT

Office/Desk

☐ Functions of other workers situated nearby
☐ Policies regading pictures, plants, and other personal items
☐ Supplies—type, location, procedures for obtaining
☐ Equipment—proper use, procedures for repair
☐ Telephone directory
☐ Phone system—dialing out, putting calls on hold, conference calls, inside calls
☐ Location of rest rooms, water fountains, break room
☐ File sign-out procedure
☐ Medical care—emergency and nonemergency

setting mutually agreed upon goals at thirty days and then at ninety days.

After two weeks, Ellen and the others who had started their new jobs on the same day were invited to a four-hour formal session that was held once a month and included new employees who had been hired by other departments in the company. The purpose of this session was to acquaint new employees with each other and with company policies and benefits not previously discussed. The vice-president of human resources, Anita Powell, welcomed the group, which consisted of twenty-five new employees, made some introductory remarks, and showed a fifteen-minute video presentation on the history of the company and the company's products and services. Top management and assorted division managers and supervisors throughout the company were featured and provided a larger framework for understanding the scope of LL International's business. Company policies and procedures that had been discussed briefly by Mr. Barnes in the smaller meeting on the first day of work, such as discipline, rules and regulations, and the company's grievance procedure, "A Fair Shake for All," were explained in more detail. Employee handbooks were distributed and employees instructed to use them as a reference. Ms. Powell answered a few questions posed by some of the participants, and then the session was adjourned.

One month after the new employees' first day of work, Mr. Barnes dropped by for an informal visit with each one of them. He checked with Ellen to see if she had any questions that remained unanswered or that she may not have felt comfortable about asking her supervisor. At the next available opportunity, he obtained a progress report from her supervisor. According to Ellen's supervisor, she had "taken like a duck to water" to her new position.

Bio-Med Corporation

"I was pleased to learn that you have accepted the position of director of finance. We were unanimous in our agreement that you are the best candidate," the director of human resources said to Jane Duffy on her first day of work. "Welcome to Bio-Med."

Jane reported to the human resources department at Bio-Med Corporation, a 10,000-employee medical equipment manufacturer located in the southwestern United States, at 7:00 A.M. to allow enough time for the director of human resources to review the company benefit plan with her and to complete all her employment paperwork.

At 8:30 A.M., she had breakfast with the executive vice-president, Martin Everett. After breakfast, he took her to her office and introduced her to her secretary. Then he and Jane sat in her office and reviewed the following orientation program he had set up for her (see box on page 77).

Having a clear idea of what her first week's activities would be, Jane eagerly went to her first meeting with the company's senior management team. Each person reviewed his or her area of responsibility and current projects and priorities. After lunch with other senior executives, Jane was introduced to her staff. Appointments had been made for her to meet individually with different members of her staff that afternoon and for part of the next day.

After completing all the individual meetings with her staff, Jane met with the executive vice-president to review the current top priorities of her department. She spent the balance of the day scheduling and conducting meetings with the key staff assigned to those activities so that she could gain a total picture of where to proceed with her responsibilities.

Over the course of that first week Jane met with the accounting partner responsible for Bio-Med's account, the company's banker, and the corporate attorney. She was quickly brought up to speed on the company's accounting practices, cash flow situation, and outstanding legal matters. At home in the evenings she reviewed policy manuals and other relevant information.

ORIENTATION SCHEDULE FOR JANE DUFFY DIRECTOR OF FINANCE WEEK OF JANUARY 4–8

Date	Activity
1/4	Company and department tour
1/4	Meeting with senior management (Bill Soderman, George Lurie, Kenneth Maynor, Sharon Melbourne, Elaine Kent)
1/4	General staff meeting—finance department (Craig Gunther, Mary Styles, Susan Bellingham, Greg Knott, Lorne Sedgewick, Gary Ripley)
1/4	Individual meetings with finance department staff (Styles, Sedgewick, Knott)
1/5	Individual meetings with finance department staff (Bellingham, Gunther, Ripley)
1/5	Overview of finance department priorities (with Martin Everett)
1/6	Priorities meeting (Bellingham, Styles, Sedgewick)
1/6	Meet with corporate attorney (David Ransom)
1/6	Meet with CPA (Josh Waverly)
1/7	Meet with banker (Kathleen Courtney)
1/8	Visit with president (John Dunham)

Optional Activities

☐ Attend general orientation session (within first two weeks)
☐ Meet with Systems Services Division

Signature: _____ Date: _____
      Jane P. Duffy, Director of Finance

Signature: _____ Date: _____
      Martin J. Everett, E.V.P.

By the second week, her initial orientation was complete and Jane was functioning as a director. The areas that she covered with the director of human resources and the orientation schedule devised by her boss were documented and placed in her personnel file.

LOVEGUEST HOTELS

Kevin Blandings was hired as a rooms division management trainee for Loveguest Hotels, a hotel chain with 150 hotels in the United States and Europe. Loveguest's management trainee program involved an extensive orientation not only to the trainee's specific department but to the hotel's other operations as well. On his first day at work, Kevin reported to the executive offices of the Chicago Loveguest, where the resident manager and director of human resources, Bruce Burkett, met him, ushered him into his office, and reviewed with Kevin his orientation program, which would last approximately three months.

Bruce Burkett explained that in his role as counselor, he would supervise Kevin and be his day-to-day guide in becoming oriented to the policies and practices of the Chicago location and to those of the Loveguest Hotel chain. Kevin's regional director of the rooms division, whose office was at international headquarters in Washington, D.C., would act as his orientation monitor. The monitor's responsibility was to provide Kevin with the big picture of the Loveguest Hotel Corporation by coordinating his corporate orientation.

The schedule on pages 79–80 was reviewed with Kevin.

The director of human resources took Kevin to the human resources office and gave him a packet of benefits and payroll enrollment materials for management trainees that had been sent from international headquarters. She explained that because he was a management trainee, his benefits and pay would be coordinated through international headquarters until he was assigned permanently to a hotel in the Loveguest chain. She outlined with Kevin his benefits entitlement and

ORIENTATION SCHEDULE AND DEPARTMENT ASSIGNMENTS LOVEGUEST HOTELS

Employee name: _____ Kevin Blandings _____

Hotel assigned to: _____ Chicago _____

Counselor: _____ Bruce Burkett _____

Monitor: _____ Elliot Adams _____

Position: _____ Rooms trainee _____

Telephone: _____ 555-8745 _____

Position: _____ Resident Manager _____

Position: _____ Regional Rooms Director _____

Orientation Schedule

Assignment	Date	Location
Report to hotel/ begin operations manual	2/12	Chicago
Begin rooms division manual	2/19	Chicago
Rotation to other divisions: Accounting	2/21–2/28	Chicago
Marketing and sales	3/3–3/10	Chicago
Engineering	3/13–3/20	Chicago
Human resources	3/23–3/30	Chicago
Food and beverages	4/2–4/9	Chicago

(continues)

Tour of food operations	4/12	International HQ
Tour of corporate offices	4/13	International HQ
Permanent assignment	On or about 4/15	TBD

payroll policies and procedures. When all the paperwork was completed, she returned Kevin to Bruce Burkett.

As Bruce and Kevin toured the hotel and Bruce introduced Kevin around, Kevin's immediate impression, based on everyone's enthusiastic greetings, was that everyone on the property had been notified of his arrival. The butterflies in his stomach settled down. At the end of the first day, he had met the other members of the executive committee—the controller, the director of marketing, the chief engineer, and the general manager. He looked forward to his second day, when he would be introduced to the rooms division staff, have an opportunity to talk with them, and be able to observe their work.

As the months passed, Kevin found everyone to be as helpful and supportive as they had been on the first day. Bruce Burkett never seemed too busy to answer any of Kevin's questions. He and Bruce frequently ate lunch together in the hotel's employee cafeteria, which gave Kevin an opportunity to discuss any insights he had had or resolve any concerns that cropped up.

At the end of the three months, Kevin was fully up to speed on rooms division operations and was ready for his first full management assignment.

PART

III

ORIENTATION
AS AN
ONGOING
ACTIVITY

CHAPTER 7

EVALUATING AND FOLLOWING UP YOUR PROGRAM

The orientation process is not complete until you have evaluated the methods and results of the program and have fine-tuned it accordingly.

Your program evaluation is done on two levels:

1. *In terms of its content and presentation methods*—whether the scope of material covered and the type of presentation materials, presenters, and audiovisual aids are appropriate.
2. *In terms of the overall results of your program*—whether the orientation has met the stated goals and objectives; that is, whether it has had a positive effect on profits, sales, costs, product or service quality, and turnover rates.

As you evaluate the orientation program at the first level, you will find that obtaining feedback can be done more informally than when you conducted your original needs assessment for developing the program. It is also more focused around the individuals most closely involved in the orientation—employees, supervisors, and the person conducting the orientation. These individuals are the best sources of information for evaluating your program. Each views the orientation program and sessions from a different perspective that will help you more accurately to determine what revisions and enhancements are necessary.

Here are some ways for you to obtain the feedback you need:

(Text continues on page 87.)

ORIENTATION PROGRAM EVALUATION

Date: _____   Your Department: _____

Presenter: _____   Your Name: _____

1. Which section of the orientation program is most important in helping you to meet the needs of your job? Check one.
   ☐ Organization history, culture and mission, function
   ☐ Seminar: "Service Is Everyone's Business"
   ☐ Work schedules and work rules
   ☐ Policies, rules and regulations, discipline and grievance procedures
   ☐ Compensation and benefits
   ☐ Performance review schedule
   ☐ Safety and emergency procedures
   ☐ Other _____
   fill in

2. State in one sentence what our business is about.

   _____

   _____

   _____

3. Rate your overall impressions on a scale of 1 (worst) to 5 (best) of the following:
   ___ Quality of visuals
   ___ Lighting
   ___ Overall physical comfort
   ___ Ventilation
   ___ Room size and setup

4. Having participated in the orientation program, are you better able to:

	Yes	No
Explain what the company does?	☐	☐
Openly discuss your concerns or suggestions with your supervisor?	☐	☐
Name the key personnel of the company?	☐	☐
Describe how your job relates to other jobs in your department?	☐	☐
Describe how your department functions in relationship to the rest of the company?	☐	☐
Perform your job tasks without first asking for instructions?	☐	☐
Act appropriately in emergency situations (fire, hurricane, earthquake)?	☐	☐
Handle customer complaints to the satisfaction of the customer?	☐	☐
Develop career goals and a personal action plan?	☐	☐

5. Which benefits that the company offers are most important to you? (Check however many apply.)

Insurance programs
☐ Life insurance
☐ Disability benefits
☐ Medical cover-
age
☐ Dental plan

☐ Vacation
☐ Holidays
☐ Sick days

☐ Tuition reimbursement
☐ Employee assistance program
☐ Career development

(continues)

6. Was there enough time allowed for this part of the orientation?

☐ Yes   ☐ No

Explain _____

_____

_____

_____

_____

7. How would you rate the orientation leader?

☐ Excellent   ☐ Fair
☐ Good   ☐ Poor

Explain your rating _____

_____

_____

_____

_____

8. To what extent were you involved in the orientation?

☐ Highly involved   ☐ Slightly interested
☐ Moderately in-   ☐ Not much interested
   terested

Explain _____

_____

_____

_____

9. What suggestions do you have for improving the orientation session?

_____

_____

_____

_____

10. Would you refer friends for positions here?

☐ Yes   ☐ No

Explain _____

_____

_____

_____

_____

1. Ask participants to complete evaluation forms like the one in the box on pages 84–87 at the end of the orientation session.

2. Ask supervisors to attend the general orientation sessions periodically to observe the program and offer their feedback. The frequency of their attendance should be in line with the number of employees from their respective departments who are oriented within a certain period of time, but should be no less than once a year. The questionnaire on pages 88–89 can be given to supervisors prior to the orientation to show them what to look for as they observe the session, but it can also be administered after they have attended.

QUESTIONS FOR LINE MANAGERS AND SUPERVISORS

1. Have you attended the new employee orientation session within the last month?

   ☐ Yes   Reason _____

   ☐ No   Reason _____

2. Rate your overall impressions on a scale of 1 (worst) to 5 (best) of the following:
   ___ Quality of visuals
   ___ Adequacy of ventilation
   ___ Lighting
   ___ Room size and setup
   ___ Overall physical comfort

3. How useful were the videotapes and printed materials to the new employee(s) and to the person responsible for the orientation?
   ☐ Very useful
   ☐ Useful to some, but not all
   ☐ Useful to most
   ☐ Not useful at all

   Explain _____

   _____

   _____

   _____

   _____

4. What, if anything, needs to be changed to make the orientation more effective? _____

   _____

   _____

_____

_____

5. Please identify two or three behaviors of the new employee showing that the orientation program did or did not convey the appropriate information.

_____

_____

_____

_____

3. Ask presenters to monitor their reactions and the reactions of the participants to what is being presented during each session. An effective presenter knows when the material is appropriate and if the message is being received. Presenters who conduct orientation sessions infrequently (three to four times a year) should complete a questionnaire (see box on pages 90–91) after each session. Those who conduct orientations more frequently (weekly or monthly) can complete a questionnaire once a month to every three months. This allows sufficient time for them to gain a broader picture of what is taking place during the session.

4. After new employees have been on the job for one month, ask them to complete a written questionnaire that lists orientation basics—key policies, procedures, benefits, and other pertinent rules and regulations. By carefully tracking their responses, you can identify which parts of the orientation presentation appear to provide the right information and which parts may need fine-tuning.

5. After new employees have been with the company for ninety days, discuss each ninety-day performance ap-

(Text continues on page 92.)

QUESTIONS FOR PRESENTERS

1. On a scale of 1 (low) to 5 (high), rate the sections of the orientation program as to their level of interest to the participants. Also note (in the Comments section) any topics that you think should be added or eliminated.

   ☐ Organization history, culture and mission, function
   ☐ Key company personnel
   ☐ Relationship of functions, departments, and jobs
   ☐ Work schedules and work rules
   ☐ Policies, rules and regulations, discipline and grievance procedures
   ☐ Compensation and benefits
   ☐ Performance review schedule
   ☐ Safety and emergency procedures
   ☐ Promotion and training opportunities
   ☐ Other _____
   ☐ Other _____
   Comments:

2. Rate your overall impressions on a scale of 1 (low) to 5 (high) on the following environmental factors:
   ☐ adequacy of ventilation
   ☐ lighting
   ☐ room size and setup
   ☐ overall physical comfort
   ☐ refreshments

3. Indicate below which visual aids you use most often and rate their effectiveness on a scale of 1 (low) to 5 (high).

                                    Rating
   ☐ video   _____
   ☐ slides   _____
   ☐ flipcharts   _____

Rating

☐ posters _____

☐ organization
chart _____

☐ overhead trans-
parencies _____

☐ other _____ _____
identify

4. Is the time allotted for presenting the program adequate?

☐ Yes ☐ No

Explain _____

_____

_____

_____

5. List any presentation techniques you use (for example, "icebreakers," guest speakers, small discussion groups) that you feel convey orientation information more effectively than the techniques used in the orientation session.

_____

_____

_____

_____

6. What suggestions do you have for improving the orientation session?

_____

_____

_____

_____

To do something better, you must work an extra bit harder.

—MIKHAIL GORBACHEV

praisal with the supervisor who gave it to determine how well the employee has adjusted to the new work environment, as demonstrated by his or her attitude, job knowledge, and productivity.

You should monitor all responses you receive over a period of from six months to one year and then review them as a whole. If hiring activity at your company is high and you conduct frequent orientation sessions, you should conduct your follow-up activities every six months. If you conduct orientations infrequently, or if your program is massive and is disseminated throughout many units of the company, following up your program may not make sense until a year or more after it is put into place.

Study and compile the results of your surveys, questionnaires, and any informal polling or feedback that you have on hand to help you evaluate your program in the light of its content, methods, and results.

CONTENT

To evaluate program content, ask yourself the following questions:

1. *Is the overall orientation program well-structured, balanced, and complete?*

   - Have we clearly conveyed our company traditions and culture? For example, is the image we project to new employees that of a conservative, "pin-stripe" company with an exacting style, or is our image that of a cutting-edge, go-ahead, informal organization?
   - Does the program have a central theme that reflects the mission and goals of the company? Are we getting across that "The customer comes first," or that we want to be "The best, not the biggest"?

The most important reason for our success is we set our objectives and make sure we follow through on them.

—ANNETTE BENETEAU ROUX

- In what ways is this theme clearly communicated to employees? Does our presentation script communicate it? What does the presence or absence of senior management at orientation sessions convey?
- Are there topics on which there is too much or too little emphasis? Is too much time spent discussing company history and not enough time devoted to what the employee can expect from the company?

2. *How do we best communicate that each person's job and work unit are tied into the larger organizational structure?*

- Do people clearly understand how their individual jobs fit in with their departments, with other departments and functions, and with the overall goals and objectives of the company?
- If we asked employees to locate their positions on the organization chart, would they be able to do so?

3. *Do we clearly distinguish between the information the new employee* must *know on the first day of work and the kind of information that can be picked up later?*

- What information should be given to new employees after the first day or week of work?
- Precisely when should this information be given?

4. *Is the overall tone of the orientation session friendly and comfortable?*

METHODS

Evaluating the efficacy of your orientation methods requires a similar set of questions:

1. *Are the sessions run in a way that reflects the mores and character of the company?* For instance, are they fast-

paced, or is the style more relaxed? Does the program follow a strict agenda, or is the format flexible within certain parameters?

2. *Are the audiovisuals of high quality?*

- Are slides, videos, posters, or charts easy to see, legible, and self-explanatory?
- Are they realistic and do they accurately reflect employees' work situations?
- Are soundtracks synchronized with the visuals and balanced in volume so that they do not drown out the accompanying narrative? Is the dialogue simple and easy to understand?
- Is the background music appropriate to the message of the audiovisual? For instance, if the objective of the audiovisual is to create enthusiasm among participants, you want music that is upbeat, perhaps the theme from *Rocky*.
- Is the information presented by the audiovisuals up to date?
- Can audiovisuals be used easily by presenters, or must you rely on someone with technological expertise?
- Are audiovisuals gender-free and do they adequately represent the diversity of the work force?
- Can audiovisuals be adapted to the needs of disabled participants through closed captions or sound vibration techniques?
- Is there content that can best be conveyed by an audio or visual? Who the key senior executives are and what they look like, where company buildings are located, and what satisfied customers say about our product or service all lend themselves to this treatment.
- At what points in the program might audiovisuals help to pick up the pace and stimulate interest?

3. *Are there any physical factors, such as inadequate ventilation, poor lighting, small room size, or noise, that detract*

*from your ability to conduct the sessions and from the
overall effectiveness of the orientation program?*

4. *Is the time allotted for the general orientation adequate to
cover all the important points?*

5. *How well do orientation session presenters communicate
with participants?*

   • Are they able to develop rapport with participants
     and command their respect? Do they convey an
     appropriate sense of humor? Are they able to pro-
     mote enthusiasm?

   • Do they use simple terminology and speak at an
     appropriate speed, and do they avoid talking down
     to new employees?

   • Do they present a credible image of themselves
     and of the company?

   • Are their presentations so organized that they can
     avoid skipping around from topic to topic?

   • Are their presentations flexible when required, as
     during video breakdowns or garbled audio por-
     tions?

   • Do presenters know how to use audiovisuals cor-
     rectly? If not, what can be done to help them learn
     to do so?

RESULTS

When you have completed your surveys, the next step is to
draw conclusions based on the results that emerge and decide
where to fine-tune the program. For example, a major
insurance company conducts a follow-up of its orientation
program one year after implementing it. Here are some of
the conclusions it reached:

The company did a study of new employees who were part
of its fast-track program for highly talented college graduates. Part of their orientation program included meetings
with top executives during the first six months of employment. Survey information revealed that doing this was pre-

mature and therefore not meaningful to recent college graduates. Instead, they wanted this feature in the second year of the program.

The evaluation process reinforced the importance of the creators' original design guidelines, which had been constructed after a careful assessment of needs and with much input from the managerial staff.

Changes in company leadership and priorities over the years pointed to the limited shelf life of the program and to the necessity for updates of videotaped and written materials.

Furthermore, the company discovered that in its zeal to cover all the bases, it had come up with a program that was much too complex. Designed to be a year-long process, with the bulk of the information presented in three to four months, the program proved formidable and uninviting. There was far too much information to be presented and also too many instructions about how to use it. The inevitable result was that managers were reluctant to use the program at all.

What managers wanted was an orientation program that:

- Fosters pride in belonging to a quality company.
- Creates an awareness of the scope of the company's business and its impact as a major financial institution.
- Emphasizes that focusing on the customer and service constitutes a competitive advantage.
- Decreases the anxieties of new employees associated with the new job.
- Helps speed the development of a contributing team member.
- Clarifies the standards of quality by which performance is measured.
- Establishes that the responsibility for personal growth and development are shared by the employee and management.

In line with what it learned from the study, the insurance company made a number of changes and refinements in its orientation program. It placed less emphasis on technical knowledge and strategies for orienting its new college graduates and focused more on their learning their way around their own departments and their roles within them during the first six months. For example, when the company obtained a large new client, it became more important for claims processors to know how to process claims than to be conversant with the company's marketing strategy.

It reduced the modular videotape program from eight tapes to two to simplify the managers' use of it. And it reduced the *Manager's Guide to Orientation* created for the program from eighty pages to sixteen.

Finally, new employees were given responsibility for their own orientation. The *Manager's Guide* is now given out both to the new employee and to the manager. On the first day of work, the employee simply takes the guide to the manager and begins the orientation process outlined in the book.

Evaluating the results of the overall orientation program is an exercise that is broader in scope than evaluating its content or methodology because you must consider whether you have met the goals and objectives of the program in the context of your company's business objectives.

Your company may have set as its goals and objectives to do the following:

- Increase productivity
- Expand market share
- Reduce turnover
- Shorten new employee acclimation time
- Increase customer satisfaction levels

You must determine how the content, methods, and final results of your orientation program have supported or not supported these goals and objectives. Here is an example:

Suppose your company has as one of its objectives "to achieve a 99 percent overall customer service rating by the end of the fiscal year." Some questions to ask in evaluating how well the orientation program has met this objective are:

1. Do employees demonstrate an understanding of the importance of customer service?

2. To what extent does every employee believe customer service is part of his/her job?
3. Do employees know where to go when they need answers to questions or other information that will help to satisfy the customer?
4. Do employees exhibit a willingness to help customers? Do they approach customers promptly and courteously? Do employees demonstrate a sincere interest in customer problems?
5. If our employees were customers, would they buy our product or use our service? How would they describe their treatment as customers? Would they recommend our product or service to others?

ORIENTATION: AN ONGOING PROCESS

Once you have completed the evaluation process, identified areas needing improvement, and fine-tuned where necessary, you have almost come full circle in the design and implementation of your orientation program. However, your orientation program will not be a completely integral part of your company's business strategy unless you include a plan to:

1. *Inform longer-term employees about topics that are covered with new employees in the orientation sessions.* Co-workers constantly share information with one another. You must make sure that information is communicated consistently to everyone to avoid morale and productivity problems.

2. *Reorient all employees annually about current and future business plans.* Your company has invested a considerable amount of time and money in the orientation program. To ensure that employees continue to be productive in their jobs to meet current business needs, you must make them aware of changes that are occurring in the company and in the company's plans for the future. It is at this point that the focus of your orientation program should move from information about the internal workings of the company to information about the company's position in the external

world. Your annual orientation updates should address these key points:

- Changes that have occurred in the past year, including business conditions that have had an impact on the company, its products, marketing strategy, or profits; key personnel changes; the introduction of new employees and/or departments; and any changes in company policies and procedures.
- The nature of the competition—its strengths and weaknesses, where the company stands in relation to the competition, and how the company plans to enhance its competitive position.
- How the company is perceived by its customers, its competitors, Wall Street, special interest groups, and the general public.
- The introduction of new markets, products, services, and customers.
- External influences on the company such as stock market fluctuations, foreign trade, or global conflict.
- Employee-related issues such as benefits, employee assistance programs, career development, and so on.
- What the company and its employees must do in the coming year to create and sustain success.
- The future—where the company sees itself going.

When your employees have a clear picture of where and how they fit into the organization, of what contribution they make, and of where their organization fits into the larger world, you have established a true orientation process.

CHAPTER 8

KEYS TO A SUCCESSFUL ORIENTATION PROGRAM

Creating a well-designed orientation process and program that achieves the objectives of high employee morale and productivity requires the willingness to invest time and money and a commitment to helping new employees make an important workplace transition.

There are certain elements essential to successful orientation programs that apply to any type of organization, large or small, and to any function or level of job. So whether you are designing a new program or revamping an existing one, remember the following do's:

1. *Make sure your program fits with the company's mission statement and its business goals and objectives.* Emphasize communicating these to employees in a relevant way. Employees need to know not only about the company's business, values, and future plans but also about where they fit in to ensure that these goals are carried out.

2. *Be sure that everyone in the organization is aware of the importance of the orientation program in maintaining and improving productivity and profits.* A solid orientation program that teaches new employees where they and their jobs fit in is the basis for any productivity efforts.

3. *Involve senior management in developing and, in some instances, participating in the actual presentation of the orientation program.* The momentum and enthusiasm generated by your program is in direct proportion to the degree of top management support and involvement.

Put your best foot forward.

—**WILLIAM CONGREVE**

4. *Give the ultimate responsibility for orienting new employees to line managers and supervisors.* In addition to making sure that new employees know the job and standards expected of them and that they are properly introduced to their work environment, supervisors should also have a clear understanding of the rationale behind the overall orientation process and of their own role in it. This has a significant impact on the long-term success of new employees.

5. *Recognize that the time between the employee's acceptance of the job and his or her start date is part of orientation.* It is during this time that the new employee begins to feel the mixed emotions of excitement and anxiety. It is important to maintain contact with new employees through letters confirming employment and welcoming letters or phone calls.

6. *Avoid information overload.* Limit the topics covered in the orientation session to high-priority subjects, such as company history and goals, employee benefits, and key rules and regulations. Consider having employees complete benefits enrollment forms and other employment documents before attending the formal orientation session.

7. *Have everything prepared for the new person's arrival on the job.* Be sure that actual work (*not* "busy work") is ready and waiting for new employees so that they do not become bored or discouraged at the outset. New employees form lasting impressions about an organization on their first day at work, and when these impressions are negative, they become candidates for early turnover, sometimes within the first sixty to ninety days of employment. Therefore, it is important that the first day of work be well-planned so that new employees feel that they have made the right choice in joining your company.

8. *Give new employees time to learn the basics—the how's, why's, and wherefores of getting things done—before starting them on their regular assignments.* Make sure that work assignments follow a logical progression so that new employees do not become overwhelmed or confused on their first day.

9. *Be sufficiently attentive to new employees during their first few days on the job to demonstrate that the company cares about*

The quality of employees will be directly proportional to the quality of life you maintain for them.

—Charles E. Bryan

their success. Taking new employees to lunch, having an open door when they have questions, and setting mutually agreed-upon performance goals shows new employees that you are as concerned about their direction in the company as they are.

10. *Orient new employees consistently.* If new employees do not come on board often and it is weeks or months before there are enough people to form a group, you should orient each new employee individually on the first day of work. Building flexibility into your orientation program allows for these individual situations and prevents sporadic or scatter-shot orientations.

11. *Follow up and review your program systematically and frequently to determine whether the program goals and objectives are being met.* This will allow you to make the necessary adjustments.

12. *Recognize that orientation is an ongoing process that involves all employees.* A well-designed orientation program does more than help new employees to adjust to the company culture. It also keeps longer-term employees informed and helps all employees to understand the company's relationship to the external world by reorienting them annually.